MW00695402

T..._

DEBT

TERMINATOR

AND WEALTH ACCUMULATOR

HOW TO:

GET-OUT-OF-DEBT AND....
GET RICH....BEYOND YOUR WILDEST DREAMS!

ABRAHAM BROWN *with Donna Gordon-Brown*

Published by: NET-TECH Communications, Inc.
Richfield, OH www.debtterminatorbook.com

Edit & design: *Monique L. Ogletree, PhD, & Nikaya D. Brown, MBA
with Leon "Trey" Haley, III*

This book is printed on acid-free paper in the United States of America by:
Fidlar Doubleday, Inc.
6255 Technology Avenue
Kalamzoo, MI 49009

Library of Congress Cataloging-in-Publication Data

Abraham Brown with Donna Gordon-Brown.
The Debt Terminator and Wealth Accumulator: How to get out of debt and get rich / Abraham Brown with Donna Gordon-Brown / NET-TECH Communications
p. cm.

ISBN 0-9769343-0-2

FIRST EDITION

Editing & cover designed by **Monique L. Ogletree**, PhD with
Leon "Trey" Haley III & **N. D. Brown,** MBA
of Tri Destined Media Enterprises

FOR MORE INFORMATION ABOUT *THE DEBT TERMINATOR & WEALTH ACCUMULATOR*
Books, computerized program for budget planning & 30-year Pay Yourself First analysis
1-330-659-3837   fax: 1-330-659-9248   www.debtterminatorbook.com

WARNING—DISCLAIMER

This book is intended to provide information regarding indebtedness and suggested options for dealing with debt. Additionally, this book shares information on the subject of wealth and its acquisition. It is sold with the understanding that the publisher and authors are not engaged in rendering legal, accounting or other professional services. If legal or other expert assistance is needed, the services of a competent professional should be sought.

Every effort has been made to make this book as accurate as possible. However, there may be mistakes, both typographical and in content. Therefore, this text should be used only as a general guide and not the ultimate authority.

The purpose of this book is to educate and entertain. The Authors and NET-TECH Communications, Inc. shall have neither liability nor responsibility to any person or entity with respect to any loss or damage caused, or alleged to have been caused, directly or indirectly, by the information contained in this book.

MONEY IS QUITE PLENTIFUL TO THOSE WHO UNDERSTAND THE *RULES* OF ITS ACQUISITION

7 RULES OF MONEY ACQUISITION

1. PAY YOURSELF FIRST 10% OF YOUR GROSS INCOME

2. MAKE YOUR DWELLING A PROFITABLE INVESTMENT

3. MAKE YOUR MONEY WORK FOR YOU EVERY DAY

4. MAINTAIN AN UNWAVERING DESIRE AND PASSION FOR THE PURSUIT OF MONEY

5. CONTROL YOUR EXPENDITURES AND BE A SAVER

6. INCREASE YOUR ABILITY TO EARN AND INSURE A FUTURE INCOME FOR YOURSELF AND YOUR FAMILY

7. GUARD YOUR MONEY FROM LOSS AND SEEK WISE COUNSEL FROM COMPETENT AND WEALTHY PEOPLE

READ ON FOR MORE WISDOM ABOUT MONEY!

DEDICATION

Recognizing that with God all things are possible and achievable, we dedicate this book to God, *"The Giver"* of all good and perfect things. I will be eternally thankful and grateful to Him for all the blessings and the tremendous favor He has shown me and my family.

To my beautiful wife, *Miss Donna*, the woman of my dreams and my very best friend, I dedicate this book, and my life to you. When God chose to bless my life with you, He gave me his greatest blessing. You complete me. Your love, your encouragement and your unwavering belief in me have made me the man I am today. I adore you and I love you.

To my three children *Monique, Nikaya (ND)* and *Charles*, I love you unconditionally. You have made me so very proud of you and your accomplishments, and I would like to thank each of you for dedicating your lives to excellence. Being your dad has been my great pleasure.

To my very good and trusted friend of more than 40 years, *Edgar Crook* and his lovely wife, *Pinky*. A friend, such as you have been to me, is truly an amazing favor and an awesome blessing from God. I thank God every day for you; one who has always been there to encourage me in the good times and in the times that weren't so good. I love you, and may God continue to bless your life abundantly is my prayer.

To some very special people that I greatly admire and who have had a considerable and lasting influence on my life - **Oprah Winfrey, Bill Cosby, Tavis Smiley, Mark Burnett,** CEO **Barbara Byrd-Bennett,** Judge **George W. Cannon,** Commissioners **Gordon A. Finch and Leonard B. Jackson.**

To two of my high school teachers who came through for me at a most crucial time in my young life. They are no longer with us, but God sent them to my aid when I had no one and nowhere to turn. Professors **Coates** and **Shiloh** were my guardian angels and I strive every day to model my life after theirs; making sure to help those who can't help themselves and allowing God to use my life for his service. I thank God for them and their lives.

Finally, to my family, Mom & Dad (**Roxie** & **Ollie Brown** who are no longer with us), **Brothers** & **Sisters (Irene, Tenna, Emma, James and Ollie II)** and a very special lady and dear friend, **Sallie J. Brown.** Thank you for helping me grow from a boy into a man. I am eternally grateful.

ACKNOWLEDGMENTS

Nothing really great ever happens without God's help! We believe that God sends caring and dedicated people to assist and encourage us along the way. We want to extend our personal and sincere thanks to some very special people who were sent to assist us:

Pastor Rev. Dr. Ronald J. Fowler & Rev. Dr. Diana L. Swoope Your insightful creation of a Debt-Free Living Ministry at the Arlington Church of God has blessed so many. Without your great vision and genuine support, this project would not have been possible. Miss Donna and I thank you for allowing us to serve and be a blessing to others. You both are so very special to us and we admire and love you immensely.

Our Students who have attended our Debt-Free Living classes and seminars - your love, your loyalty, your enthusiasm, your encouragement and your hunger for financial wisdom had great influence on our final decision to write this book. Your unrelenting encouragement and the tremendous financial growth that we have observed as a result of your application of our debt-free living concepts; helped us recognize the critical need for this how to get-out-of-debt book. We thank you all so very much!

Antoinette Bell, Diane Henderson, Bernadette Salley, Janish Ogletree, Anne Sojourner, Belinda Hinton, Timothy Ramsey, Larry Young, Arthur Barkley, Nolen Fitzpatrick and the late *Rev. Howard C. Berry* - for your unwavering enthusiasm and constant encouragement at times when we needed it the most.

N.D. Brown, MBA – CEO Tri Destined Studios - for the many hours of editing and getting us prepared to take our message of financial empowerment and deliverance to the four corners of the world. Your ideas relative to a "DEBT TERMINATOR" Reality TV Show" based on the concepts embraced in this book could bless millions. My dearest daughter, your global vision for this kind of inspired message is God sent. God needs us to think and dream big when setting out to help and bless others. We will trust this ground-breaking mission to you and your expert team at Tri Destined Studios in Hollywood. Just thinking of you and your enduring passion to help others, brings me great joy.

Monique L. Ogletree, PhD - Baylor College of Medicine Texas Children's Hospital - for the endless number of hours spent correcting and editing my rough draft manuscript to ensure that it is of an acceptable quality for our readers. My dearest daughter, finally, all of my past investments in your exceptional education are starting to payoff. I'm so proud of you and the extremely critical heart research work you do on behalf of children around the world. Your outstanding con-tributions will positively affect the young lives of so many.

CONTENTS

PART TWO: *GETTING OUT OF DEBT*

PART THREE: *ACCUMULATING WEALTH*

INTRODUCTION

Our environment plays a major role in shaping our physical as well as our mental behavior. What and how we think, what we believe and what we eventually achieve in our lives is largely the results of what our parents thought and believed; what religious background we hailed from; what educational influences we encountered along the way; and oh yes, who our friends and peer groups were from our birth to this very moment. If a person comes from a poor or middle class environment, his values and beliefs relative to money could be indifferent and distorted. You see, we humans have an innate and intrinsic ability to justify and/or rationalize the position or predicament in which we find ourselves; particularly if we can see very little hope for change in our dilemma. Thus, we learn to live with it; so to speak. "There's no beneficial use in crying over spilled milk; just clean it up and move on".

Today, in our society the strong grip of DEBT has caused so many good and deserving people to give up on their dreams of ever becoming secure financially. Indebtedness is almost an epidemic in our country. It's a horrific disease that is causing stress, havoc and panic everywhere with no apparent end in sight. Something needs to be done. A solution of some kind must be found and implemented quickly. Debt is literally sucking all the joy out of the lives of so many, and it's time to fight back. It's time to take back control of our lives and bring back the joy and peace that we once knew. Sometimes, just a little wisdom and a few words of encouragement are all we need to enrage an unconquerable uprising against any enemy that means to cause us harm.

This book will provide you with the wisdom and a "get-out-of-debt" strategy that you have been hoping and waiting for. Together, we will explore straight-forward and practical solutions that will help you wage a powerful and inspired come-back against the indebtedness that you face. We trust that the "get-out-of-debt" strategy that you eventually choose will motivate and arouse, within you, the courage to dream and hope again. As you move forward in this text you will discover:

> **4 Options and approaches to terminate & eliminate your debt;**
> **7 Habits & Lifestyles practiced by the Rich to accumulate wealth;**
> **7 Rules & Secrets for acquiring money & wealth;**
> **7 Laws of money.**

Our fundamental mission is to share the simple and proven path that we have successfully used to acquire wealth and financial freedom. But, before we can appropriately situate you on this new and exciting path towards acquiring wealth, we may first need to assist your efforts to get-out-of-debt. Now, if you are not in debt, that's terrific and we congratulate and applaud you. And as a reward, you can get started with haste on your new and exciting journey towards acquiring wealth and the great source of pleasure that comes as a result of it. You can skip pass *"PART TWO"* which features our get-out-of-debt strategies and go directly to *"PART THREE"* and begin our lessons dealing with the accumulation of wealth. In *"PART THREE"* you'll discover some of the secrets for acquiring wealth. You'll also uncover seven significant and key **Habits and Lifestyles** that are practiced by the rich to achieve wealth. If you learn and strictly adhere to these **Habits and Lifestyles** you will be well on your way to achieving a major financial breakthrough in your life.

Before any discussions or plans regarding the acquisition of money can make a serious difference in your life, you need to first resolve your issues of indebtedness. Towards this end, we have incorporated for your use *(4) simple and proven options for eliminating debt* that are easy to understand and easy to follow. You'll be able, on your own, to choose and implement an option that will best fit your unique situation. That option, if followed and adhered to will help you get out of debt and stay out for good. Additionally, suggested lifestyle changes will be revealed that can put you and your family on an immediate path towards accumulating the wealth and financial security that you want and deserve.

Finally, we will attempt to highlight some societal problems that we feel may have facilitated and given support to widespread indebtedness and poverty in our country. Our ultimate goal here is to free the minds of a great number of people who have been mentally imprisoned and enslaved much too long because of the following societal influences:

1. **OUR ENVIRONMENT** which perpetuates and encourages many of the Habits & Lifestyles practiced by the poor and middle class.

2. **OUR PLACES OF WORSHIP** which excessively vilify the rich and thereby discourage an unwavering desire for the pursuit of money. *"For the love of money is the root of all evil"*. (Tim. 6:10)

3. **OUR SCHOOLS & INSTITUTIONS OF HIGHER LEARNING** which lack prerequisite coursework in the areas of financial instruction and training.

While not vicious or malicious in their intent, I believe their current actions and approaches are causing serious problems. Problems that are negatively impacting people financially; both, through the lack of education relative to money, and lack of encouragement relative to the pursuit of money.

To this I say, enough already:

> *Let the people go.*
> *Let them grow and prosper.*
> *Help them to learn and achieve.*
> *Show them the right way.*
> *It's their time now!!*

It is my deepest hope and my most sincere desire that you'll take the knowledge shared in this book and ***SEIZE THE MOMENT*** for yourself and those you love.

PART ONE

EXPLORING WHY IT IS, WHAT IT IS

A STORY OF HARDWORK, DESIRE & PERSISTENCE

Before I share with you the process of terminating your debt or accumulating wealth, I want to tell you a story of a little boy who actually was part of the inspiration for this book. His name is not important, but his story can be one of great motivation to anyone who finds himself or herself in a financial struggle or any struggle, for that matter, with very little hope in sight. This little boy was born in the back woods of Thomaston, Alabama in the deep south to a very poor family with eight children. Each child had chores in the fields picking cotton, bailing hay, milking cows, caring for the farm animals and all the other farm activities that required free labor. His father was a share-cropper and during the harvest season, the family would wake up at day-break, put on their rags and go to the fields; where the children helped pick cotton until it was time for the school bus. When the school day was over, the bus brought the children home and it was back to the fields to pick more cotton until the sun went down. Darkness would almost always come before they arrived at the little hut where they lived. That was the boy's life for 17 years.

One day the boy noticed that the owner of the land had short-changed his father and he mentioned it to his dad. Since his father could not read or write and was pretty much at the mercy of the rich land owner, he advised his eager and money-driven young son to keep the peace and just let it go. In those days cheating the uneducated "share-croppers" was common place. All of the rich land owners probably did it. So, the young boy watched his father being cheated for the next few years. Then he graduated from high school and his life changed forever. A few days after his graduation he went to the owner of the land and told him that he was aware of him cheating his father out of his money over all those years, and that he should do right by his father. The owner was shocked, appalled and down right angry at the accusation that he threatened to kick the whole family out if the young boy did not get off his property at once. This was not a good situation, because where was he to go at age 17? The young boy's mother begged the land owner for mercy towards her son. She offered to cook and clean his house for free for as long as it took if he would just not kick the family and her son out. No! The rich land owners said angrily, "I want that boy off my property when I return here tomorrow".

As the young boy's family pondered their predicament, his mother turned to the only real help that she knew. Weeping, she fell to her knees and started to pray and begged God to please make a way for her son. "My Lord, I have no power, but you have all power", she said. As fate would have it, on that very night, two of the young boy's high school teachers, who had been impressed with his work ethics and scholastic abilities, came to let his parents know that they had made arrangements for their son to get an early work scholarship to college, which included a room and immediate occupancy. The boy's mother, with tears running down her face, thanked God for sending His Angels to help her son. The teachers (God sent Angels) took the young boy with them that night.

What a miracle! What a blessing! With God everything is possible. God answered that mother's prayer and He showed great favor towards her young son. He must have had some divine plan for the boy's life, one could assume. The young boy's upbringing of working hard, seeking wisdom from those who knew much, and caring about the welfare of those who were less fortunate would prove to be beneficial throughout the twists and turns life would bring his way. During his senior year of college, finances and school loans finally got the best of him; so he had to drop out to get two jobs to pay-off his debts. He came to hate being in debt and the helpless and enslaved feeling he felt as a result of it. He deeply loved his parents but he wanted to make sure that his life would be different from theirs. He wanted to become someone with influence who could help others like his two teachers had helped him. He wanted to own his own land so that no one could come and kick him off like the land owner who cheated his father. He wanted to learn all he could about money and how to accumulate it so that he could teach others how to. Finally, he wanted to make his parents proud and give them a piece of the good life before they died.

In the early seventies, he landed a position in the world of computer technology where he worked as a computer salesman and sales manager for three of the largest computer firms in the world - Honeywell, Sperry Univac and DEC.

But once again, fate would have his turn of events; after 24 years of employment and becoming one of the top most sought after salespersons in the computer industry, he was down-sized. Just when he thought he had achieved financial security, old man fate was on his trail once again. He was told it wasn't personal, it was just business. Remembering the principles that had brought him success in the past, he started his own computer services business. He had also invested in real estate some years prior to being down-sized.

You see, each time life handed him a cancerous situation; he overcame through faith, perseverance, and wisdom. No matter what his circumstances were he was able to bounce back because he refused to give up on his dream of becoming financially secure. Memories of his dad having to endure the unjust treatment from the rich land owner created an unwavering desire to someday achieve great wealth. He always seeked advice from wealthy people and learned much about money matters. His sound financial dealings and money management skills became obvious to those who knew him. People began to seek his counsel. Soon members of his church and neighbors that had witnessed his tenacity to withstand financially through the years, started asking how he always had money for his family and how he could afford the finer things in life? As word of the very helpful and valuable debt free counseling began to spread, more and more people with debt issues would come to him. Finally, recognizing the tremendous benefit that a debt free living ministry could bring, the Pastor of his church asked him to teach a Sunday school class on debt free living and debt termination. The Sunday school class was quite successful and soon some colleges and universities and other social groups began to call for his no nonsense and simplified approach to financial wellness. He positively affected so many of his students that they affectionately gave him the name **"THE DEBT TERMINATOR"**.

I'm humble to acknowledge that I am *"THE DEBT TERMINATOR"* and that was my story. As you can see, my life was not an easy one. Nothing worthwhile is ever easy, so you play the cards you're dealt and give life everything you've got. You see, we cannot control the situations and circumstances that God places in our lives to make us stronger and better. Yes, I believe God did have a divine plan for my life, and I believe He's allowing me to work his plan with this book. You see, when I can teach and help others to discover a better financial existence in this life, it brings me the utmost fulfillment and the greatest joy. God wants everyone to be prosperous and happy; but each of us has his or her part to perform in the deal. Desire is the key that shapes or helps to determine our life's final outcome. When life's situations and circumstances knock us down, and they most certainly will; *how long you stay down is up to you*.

I wrote this book, not only to take you on my journey which is *a testimony of one man's rise from rags to riches;* but more importantly, *to show that if I, who was born to a family of uneducated share-croppers; who was forced away from my family and my home at age 17; who dropped out of college before graduating, could do it, SO CAN YOU.*

Remember, *when you get to the top, don't forget to send the elevator back down*.

WHY ARE WE SUCH FINANCIAL CRIPPLES? WHAT WENT SO TERRIBLY WRONG?

WORDS and PHRASES written or spoken by others deceptively create our being; they shape our mind, controlling and influencing our every thought; they imprison and incarcerate us inside an imaginary **BOX**, leading us to conclude that life only exists **"HERE IN THIS BOX"**; they destroy our creativity and our vision, leaving us to wonder aimlessly cross the wilderness and meadows of life without even questioning, WHY. WORDS of advice and guidance can be found every-where and everywhere you can find someone speaking words. Whether right or wrong, good or bad, safe or dangerous, word power permeates our world; controlling and manipulating life outcomes and life consequences of all those who participate in the passageway of WORDS.

The simple truth of the matter is everyone deserves to know what is really real. They deserve to and need to know what truly matters in the big picture of life. Our society tends to be one that encourages and prepares people to focus on and deal with the small things; while leaving the large and more important things that really matter to chance. Don't you wish the politicians and business leaders would just tell it like it is without all the fluff, deception and confusion? Wouldn't it be refreshing for our religious leaders to just tell it like it is; rather than focusing on those topics or themes which persuade the people to do things which are only good for the church with little or no regard for the financial and social needs of the people?   Don't you wish our schools would begin to teach courses that we can truly use once we enter the world of work? I've worked in the computer and technology industries for over 35 years; working 25 years with three of the largest computer manufacturing and distribution companies in the world, and worked the last 10 years in a computer and technology based company that I own.   Up to and including this very day, I have yet to require the use of Calculus, Geometry, Trigonometry, and/or Physics in my work career. Now, that's not to say that these subjects and courses serve little purpose; but, how about including prerequisite courses that focus on money management & investing and workshops that stress the importance of "paying yourself first"?   On the other hand, everyday during my 35 years of work I have been required, in one form or another, to deal with the subject of money and questions regarding its use.

Political correctness has its place and in every place you will find those who will be politically correct at all cost no matter who gets hurt. That's just the world we live in. That's what is acceptable and expected of all its citizens. And if you are seeking another politically correct book on the subject of

DEBT and the accumulation of WEALTH, you should choose another book. In this book, we will tell it like it is; the real truth and nothing but the truth. You will find this book to be straight-forward, honest and to the point. You will, for the very first time, know exactly where you stand and have concrete strategies to change your life for the better. When you know precisely where you are, you can more easily and more quickly map-out a strategy that will take you where you want to go.

My father-in-law (*Andrew Gordon*), a very wise old gentleman I might add, told me something once that I thought was quite profound when taken in its simplest context. Let me share with you what he told me. He said, *"When you learn, then you know and that's the greatest position to be in; but when you don't know, then you may have to guess, and when you have to guess, you've got a problem"*. Our educational systems have under prepared its people in the area of finances; and consequently, these unprepared people will always find themselves having to guess. Why so, because our K-12 and College curriculums lack prerequisite coursework that lend themselves to specialized instructions relative to money and finances; therefore, rarely will students of our current educational systems know the answers pertaining to money. And as my father-in-law so elegantly stated, if you don't know, you may have to guess and when you have to guess, you've got a problem. Hopefully, this book will help you to *learn* and take some of the guess-work out of the financial decisions you will be making in the future. Guessing is much like gambling! Sometimes you'll win but most often than not you will lose. Bottom-line, to be successful in finance there are certain things you need to know! And, that's the paramount reason why we wrote this book - **THE DEBT TERMINATOR & WEALTH ACCUMULATOR**. Our most important goal is to help you become more knowledgeable relative to the subject of money and financial matters.

We firmly believe that in order to make a real significant change in most people's personal financial habits and behaviors, a **RE-EDUCATION** or a **MIND-MAKE-OVER**, so to speak, is required. Put another way, in order to help most people change or improve their financial positions, it may become necessary to help them alter or revolutionize their thinking as it pertains to money and the intrinsic value of possessing it. Principally because of this fact, we have devoted a good measure of time and effort addressing this serious issue of dealing with one's mental preparation.

Miss Donna and I produce and present many Debt Free Living Classes and Seminars involving Adults, College and High School Students. We always seem to find ourselves dealing with an issue that continues to amaze and trouble us at the same time. In almost every class there is at least one or two students, who will stand and emphatically declare that they have little or no desire to become wealthy and truly could care less about money. The most frequently expressed reason for this declaration is an association of **_WEALTH AND MONEY_** with **_GREED AND EVIL_**. The Biblical Scripture: ***"FOR THE LOVE OF MONEY IS THE ROOT OF ALL EVIL"*** seems to always make its way into the class discussions. However, all the other eager participants want very much to be rich and financially independent, and not just for the sake of being wealthy people. They want to create better lives for themselves and their families. They want to be able to help somebody else along the way and to make our world a better place. Our students realize, as we do, that it's hard to make a real difference in the world in which we live without adequate financial resources. They also understand that with money they can do a lot of good. The love of money may very well be the root of all evil; however, if you look at the other side of that same coin, one could surely make the case that money is also the root or origin of all good. It should be noted, however, that by the end of our presentations, many of those persons who started out alleging no desire for money or wealth did change their position.

We have also found that when people learn the truth about money, or at least are presented another view of money, they become more comfortable with the notion that money is a good thing. It's quite obvious that many people have been misinformed and deceived about money. We have found three very destructive and devastating forces that have left a lot of people in our society mentally crippled as it pertains to finance and money matters. To identify the culprits and the roles they've played in this deception, even though not necessarily intended for harm, is necessary. Our major challenge is to create awareness of these forces in our society and to re-educate folks regarding money matters; so that they can begin their new journey on the road to wealth and prosperity.

The intent here is not to point fingers or place blame; but rather, to raise awareness on the behalf of all parties involved. We want to give assurance that money, wealth and power are all good, and we will be providing some unbiased and supporting documentation for your consideration.

Now, let's take a hard look at the three (3) forces that, we believe, are partially to blame in the making of financial cripples:

1. **OUR ENVIRONMENT**

2. **OUR CHURCHES & RELIGIOUS GROUPS**

3. **OUR INSTITUTIONS OF HIGHER LEARNING**

OUR ENVIRONMENT

Our environment is one where *spending appears to be king*. Keeping pace with the Joneses seems to be the main focus of our middle class generation. Looking successful rather than actually achieving success is a sham or role-play embraced by the poor and middle class alike. Spending their hard-earned money as fast as they earn it seems to be the practice of the great majority. Mind-sets and attitudes that support the notion that money is only made to be spent with no regard for the tomorrow, which will surely come, permeate our culture. The rich keeps getting richer while the poor keeps getting poorer and the beat goes on.

Persons found to be from poor and deprived backgrounds and who have experienced the unfortunate circumstances relative to the lack of money; represent the toughest group of individuals to reach concerning discussions having to do with the acquisition of money. One would think that a person who had so little would be the most eager to learn about the money acquisition process. Wrong!! Contrary to popular belief, this is not the case; in fact, you will find many poor people defending and holding their deprived lifestyle very dear to their way of life. Why you ask? I'm not sure; but I suspect that this may have ties to their parent's religious beliefs about the subject of money.

You see, many believed that Jesus lived a life of poverty and deprivation. And, if that lifestyle was the one chosen by our Lord and Savior, Jesus Christ, then maybe there is something sacred or blessed about it. Personally, as I envision the life of Jesus, I see one who could have had everything; one who could have been rich beyond measure.

Now, I know this will be quite a stretch for some, but let me explain how I reached this conclusion. As we all have read, Jesus could heal the sick; He could even raise the dead; He could speak to the wind and it obeyed him. On one occasion when Jesus and his disciples needed money to pay taxes, He sent Peter, one his disciples, to retrieve money from the mouth of a fish; not only that, he fed a multitude of thousands with two little fishes and five loafs of bread. That having been said, anyone processing such awesome and overwhelming powers, as did Jesus, could not possibly have been poor. Imagine the price one would pay to raise a loved one from the dead or to cure a young child of cancer.

As for our parents, being poor was never what they desired, it was perhaps just the best that they could do; given the circumstances and the challenges that they faced during their generation. Our world was a much different place when our parents came along, and opportunities for advancement and for the pursuit of money were not as widespread as they are today. It makes no logical sense for anyone to hold on to financial attitudes and viewpoints of a past generation who apparently were not afforded many good opportunities in the arena of money. *We all love our parents.* They are very good and most honorable people in nearly all instances; however, let's just be honest, many of our parents missed the boat financially. They never quite figured out how to get ahead. Those paydays never came quite fast enough. When they did get paid, they always seem to find themselves just a little short in the cash department. Our parents did their best to keep clothes on our backs, food in our bellies and a shelter over our heads. They kept us in school and out of trouble. Some of our parents even paid for our college education. Let's not forget all those parents who also paid for the weddings of their daughters. I think we can all agree that our parents are great people; but most of our parents are "broke", and in the end will probably die poor and deprived. Therefore, if we do what our poor and deprived parents did, we'll get the same results our parents got...we will end up financially deprived as well.

Poor people usually make friends with other poor people and *THE ART OF BEING POOR* is perpetuated throughout this circle of friends, and then their children take on the art of being poor and their children and on, and on. After so many generations practicing *THE ART OF BEING POOR*, it becomes their "only" way of life - an epidemic of sorts. In some religious circles, being without is sometimes seen and described as a blessing in disguise. Even though that seems so nonsensical and ridiculous, it's a fact.

If your whole family and all of your friends are poor, there's absolutely no value in getting advice about money from them. If you want to be rich, you must learn and adhere to the habits & lifestyles of the rich and break away from those habits & lifestyles of the poor and middle class.

NOT ROCKET SCIENCE, JUST COMMON SENSE!

OUR CHURCHES & RELIGIOUS GROUPS

Our **CHURCHES AND RELIGIOUS** organizations have not only been very timid on the subject of money; they have in many ways discouraged people from a strong and passionate pursuit of wealth and money. How so? We believe that there maybe misinterpretations involving some Biblical Scriptures that pertain to **MONEY & RICHES**. Some **CHURCHES and RELIGIOUS** groups tend to emphasize certain Biblical Scriptures pertaining to money and wealth as being negative and destructive; while obviously and noticeably de-emphasizing or never mentioning or focusing on other Scriptures that pertain to the positive aspects of money and wealth. Their messages seem to stress the scriptures that vilify and malign money and those who possess much of it. Believers are put in a precarious and unfair position of having to make financial lifestyle decisions relative to money, and how it could impact their relationship with other men and their God. A matter of fact, God wants us all to be rich and prosperous. God owns everything and he shares it with each of us based on our ability to do the wise things with what he shares. He even rejoices in our financial triumphs and accomplishments. (See Exhibit 1: Parable of the Talents)

To reiterate, I firmly believe that deceptive **words** and **phrases** written or spoken by others create our being; they shape our mind, controlling and influencing our every thought; they imprison and incarcerate us inside an imaginary **BOX**, leading us to conclude that life only exist **"here in the BOX";** they destroy our creativity and our vision, leaving us to wonder aimlessly cross the wilderness and meadows of life **without even questioning, why.** Words of advice and guidance can be found everywhere and everywhere you can find someone speaking words. Whether right or wrong, good or bad, safe or dangerous, word power permeates our world; controlling and manipulating life outcomes and life consequences of all those who participate in the passageway of words.

People must not lose their desire to question and to explore, even if criticism is severe. In the end, we all will be better served as a result of people having inquisitive minds. We must attempt to create a new and fresh look at how things are and how maybe they could or should be. In the final analysis, you the reader will be the judge of whether this book created, for you, a new view or a new freedom, if you will, to go after that dream that you once thought impossible. That is our hope. Remember, money does answer all things and with God all things are possible.

As previously discussed, religious philosophy can have a huge impact on your attitude towards money. Now, let's take a closer look at some Biblical Scriptures and we'll let you be the judge as to their significance on one's outlook relative to money and riches.

BIBLICAL SCRIPTURES - *EMPHASIZED AND DE-EMPHASIZED*

Emphasized Biblical Scriptures: (Money is not good - give it away)

"For the love of money is the root of all evil". (Tim. 6:10)

"God loveth a cheerful giver". (2 Cor. 9:7)

"Will a man rob God? Yet ye have robbed me. But ye say, Wherein have we robbed thee? In tithes and offerings". (Mal. 3:8)

"If thou wilt be perfect, go sell that thou hast, and give to the poor", (Rich Young Ruler meets with Jesus) (Matt. 19:21)

"It is easier for a camel to go through the eye of a needle than for a rich man to enter the kingdom of God". (Matt. 19:24) & (Mark 10:25)

DE-Emphasized Biblical Scriptures: (Accumulating Money is good & wise)

"A feast is made for laughter, and wine maketh merry: but money answerth all things". (Ecclesiastes 10:19)

"For unto everyone that hath shall be given, and he shall have abundance: but from him that hath not shall be taken away even that which he hath". (Matt. 25:29)

"Take heed how you hear; for whosoever hath, to him shall be given, and whosoever hath not, from him shall be taken even that which he seemth to have". (Luke 8:18)

"The rich ruleth over the poor, and the borrower is servant to the lender". (Proverbs 22:7)

"The poor is hated even of his own neighbor: but the rich hath many friends" (Prov. 14:20)

"With men it is impossible, but not with God, for with God all things are possible". (Matt. 19:26) & (Mark 10:27)

"In the house of the wise are stores of choice food and oil, but a foolish man devours all he has". (Proverbs 21:20)

"He that hath a bountiful eye shall be blessed". (Proverbs 22:9)

"Poverty and shame shall be to him that refuseth instruction". (Prov. 13:18)

"I am the Lord thy God which teacheth thee to profit, which leadeth thee by the way that thou shouldest go". (Isaiah 48:17)

THE BIBLE - *MISUNDERSTOOD AND MISINTERPRETED*

You may be familiar with a Biblical Scripture in the book of Matthew the 19TH Chapter, Versus 16-24 and in the book of Mark the 10TH Chapter, Versus 17-25; where you'll find Jesus as he talks to the *"RICH YOUNG RULER"* about his wealth; and then farther down into the scripture, Jesus talks with his disciples about the difficulty a rich man would have in his effort to obtain heaven. In fact, the rich man's plight for getting into heaven, at first reading, was horrendously described as a hopeless case. The scripture alluded to an *"EYE OF A NEEDLE"* and characterized a rich man's chances of getting into heaven as compared to someone pulling a camel through the *eye of that needle.*

At best, this is simply a dreadful and horrific scene for any young mind or old one, for that matter, to deal with. With this horrifying picture describing the doom and gloom that will come about as a result of being rich, one could feel it better to just be without riches and guarantee a safe and certain journey through the heavenly gates.

Many believe the Bible, in this instance, has been grossly misunderstood. First of all, that *eye of a needle* is not the type of sewing needle that immediately comes to mind; it was an opening or a gate in biblical times where the camels would enter into the city. All camels could fit through the gate or **"needle's eye"**, as it was called; but some of the larger camels with over-sized backpacks could not fit through the gate or **needle's eye** until their backpacks were removed or taken off. When the packs were taken off, the camel could go through the needle's eye or gate with no problems.

Secondly, if you read carefully the 21st Verse in the 19th Chapter of the book of St. Matthew, it reads thusly: "Jesus said unto him (Rich young ruler), *__if thou wilt be perfect,__* go and sell that thou hast, and give to the poor, and thou shalt have treasure in heaven: and come and follow me.

The issue here is: "if thou wilt be perfect" or more clearly stated: if you will or wish to be perfect then go and sell that which you have. It's very clear that none of us are perfect, only Jesus could fit that criterion. Many biblical scholars will have you believe that when the rich young ruler walked away sadden, he had condemned his soul to hell because he was unwilling to pay the ultimate price for getting into heaven. Once you read the 19th Chapter, starting with the 16th – 24th'' verses more closely and more carefully you will discover that the rich young ruler was already keeping all of

the 10 commandments ordered by God; therefore, by most religious standards he was already eligible to go to heaven.
The only issue here is "to be perfect"; and to that, the rich young ruler did not feel the price reasonable given his human needs. Remember the rich young ruler was only human as we are. How many among us would sell all we have and give it to the poor just so that we could claim to be perfect? Not many, if any, I can guarantee you that.

Just for laughs, the next time you have an opportunity to meet with some real Bible carrying Christians, I want you to pose a hypothetical notion that suggests they sell all that they have and give to the poor; and as a reward, they can claim perfection and they can then go follow Jesus and be assured a seat in the kingdom of Heaven. Tell them that they need, also, to keep all of the Ten Commandments of God. Now, be very careful to note what their reactions will be. My guess is, they would all have a similar reaction to that of the Rich Young Ruler. They will reject the notion and dismiss you as being out of your mind and some kind of lunatic, religious fanatic or extremist.

My point is, sometimes we Christians make a big deal about nothing or we place more significance on a particular situation or circumstance than is warranted. In other words, I believe we make the path to heaven narrower than God had intended for it to be. Some devout Christians have set themselves up as God's unofficial gate-keepers, and they may be scaring a lot of people away from our places of worship and our religions with this unauthorized and unsubstantiated foolishness. Why don't we just lighten up so that everyone can get a chance to experience God's awesome power. Once People get a taste of God, he will lead them where they need to go. We have taken over for God and I'm not sure that we have it right all the time. Do you remember how Jesus had to continually chastise and rebuke his Disciples because they were so critical and so overly judgmental of the people? Can you recall how the people wanted to stone that poor woman in the Bible who had been found committing adultery, and how Jesus shamed the crowd out of stoning her by making them look at themselves, who also had committed sins? He persuaded those people to lighten up on their spirit of condemnation and take on a spirit of forgiveness and understanding. No one is perfect, that's just a fact.

I find that some Christian people are much tougher on people than God would be. I have observed this kind of behavior in my own church, and you probably have also at your place of worship. I'm referring to the *"MORE HOLY THAN THOU"* attitude and behavior that you can experience with some church folks. So let's give the rich young ruler a break already and get on with bigger things that really matter.

Isn't it silly how something so simple can scare people out of their dreams? So many have been immobilized through fear of the adverse consequences pertaining to the *"after-life"*; so much so, they waste many, many golden opportunities to do well and make a difference in *"this life, here and now"*. It happens all the time. It may be happening in your life right now. If so, this book can help you start a new "fear-free", motivated, and aggressive journey in the pursuit of wealth and money.

Many believe the Bible to be the manuscript for life. Biblical teachings and illustrations are the most powerful, most believed, most adhered to and most influential literary work in our culture. It is the single most powerful influence to our way of life. Persons who represent themselves as having been chosen by God to preach the Gospel have an awesome responsibility to teach the word (Biblical Scripture); but more importantly, to make sure that their interpretations of the Biblical Scriptures are on target and is right.

Religious leaders sometimes tend to spend very little time on scriptures that applaud the ambitious performer and the rich in the Bible. For example, there is a Scripture found in the book of Matthew chapter 25, where Jesus taught his disciples the ***PARABLE OF THE TALENTS***. In this scripture, beginning at verse 14 – 29, three servants were all given talents by their master who was leaving for a prolonged trip. To the first Servant 5 talents were given; then, to the second Servant 2 talents were given; and finally, to the third servant only 1 talent was given. In reading this Biblical account for the first time, it does not appear to be a very fair and equitable transaction, particularly in the cases of the latter two Servants. What then, could Jesus possibly teach in this very seemingly unfair and unchristian like distribution arrangement? Well, after reading the whole story (Matt. 25:14-29) it become quite clear that it is God's plan and desire for us all to be rich and prosperous; and to have life and have it more abundantly. In fact, if you read that particular scripture, you will see that the master on his return celebrated the success of the first two servants; although they had been given different amounts, they both had doubled what they had been given, and thus were rewarded with increased amounts. In this **PARABLE OF THE TALENTS,** think of ***God as the Master***, and ***we as the Servants*** and the ***Talents as the Money***. The third servant was a disappointment to the master because he did not make a profit with the master's money. I believe that the **PARABLE OF THE TALENTS** demonstrates how God rejoices in, and rewards our successes and how he is not pleased when we fail because of a lack of desire or laziness. Since we know how powerful of an influence the Bible and religious leaders have on people, it should be a crime if this influence and power is intentionally misused.

This book is aimed at revealing the truth. A simplified diagram (EXHIBIT 1 - THE PARABLE OF THE TALENTS SIMPLIFIED) has been included for your examination and study. Take a few minutes to review Exhibit 1. I believe you will find it to be enlighten-ing and a somewhat different point of view from which to analyze these circumstances. Point of view can sometimes distort our vision and thinking; while on the other hand, it can aid our vision and our thinking, making things crystal clear. I am presenting "EXHIBIT 1" in hopes that it will help improve your vision and thinking as it pertains to money and how God truly regards this precious gift that he gives to each of us. Some of us take his talents (money) and we save and make it grow, which pleases God; while others take God's talents (money) and they devour it all as fast as they get it, and show total disregard for its value and the value of God "The Giver" of all good and perfect things. To spend ill-responsibly does not please God. Think of it, if you gave someone a precious and valuable gift and they just threw it away with total disregard for you or the gift, how would that make you feel? You probably would hesitate giving that person another valuable gift.

PARABLE OF THE TALENTS SIMPLIFIED
KING JAMES VERSION - *MATTHEW 25:14-29*

5 TALENTS GIVEN

INCREASED TO 10 TALENTS

MADE RULER OVER MANY THINGS!
PLUS 1 ADD'L TALENT - TAKEN FROM
WICKED & SLOTHFUL 3RD SERVANT BELOW

2 TALENTS GIVEN

INCREASED TO 4 TALENTS

MADE RULER OVER MANY THINGS!

1 TALENT GIVEN

REMAINED AT 1 TALENT

MADE RULER OVER NOTHING - EVEN
THE 1 TALENT WAS TAKEN AWAY AND
GIVEN TO THE 1ST SERVANT ABOVE

EXHIBIT 1

To undo some of the many mistaken beliefs and misinterpretations relative to the true benefits of money and the added value it can bring to a life, some individuals will need to experience a **TOTAL MIND MAKE-OVER, A PARADIGM SHIFT, IF YOU WILL.** You see, God created man to be noble and rich; yet man reduces himself to poverty primarily through foolishly spending all of the money he earns on things that become worthless over time.

Why is that?

God gives every person talents that if applied with hard work, desire and persistence, anything and everything is achievable. Why then, is it so difficult for some people to believe in themselves when they have been given everything that they need to succeed?

Allow me to share with you a very LITTLE-KNOWN BIBLICAL SCRIPTURE that has helped me to become totally comfortable and thoroughly convinced with the notion that THE PURSUIT OF MONEY is right, it is good; and it is a life changing adventure practiced by those who are wise:

A feast is made for laughter, and wine maketh merry: but MONEY ANSWERETH ALL THINGS. Eccl. 10:19 (KJV)

Since money answers all things, it makes good business sense as well as good common sense to have as much money as you possibly can. That way, no matter what happens in your life or in the lives of your family; if you have enough money, you have the answer or solution to your problem or dilemma. Plus, with money you can give God the ***ultimate gift*** - the gift of helping and blessing others.

Before we leave this topic - The Bible misunderstood and misinterpreted, let's look at God and try to better understand what He desires of us, His children. During this mission you will need to be open to a fresh and new way of looking at God. You see, you are free to make up your own mind about how you see the world and even how you see God. No one that we know has ever spoken directly to God; and therefore, what anyone believes or tells you to believe about God is just that person's take or opinion on the subject. Here's my take. It's simple and it's easy to understand. Let's start with the all important question at hand.

What does God want from us, His children?

Here's what we all know. God is love. To better understand this love phenomenon, we need to look at it in earthly terms. We need to find an early love that comes closest to that kind of love that we know God must have for us, His children.

As we go in search of this earthly love it must meet certain Godly criteria. In other words, this love must be unconditional. It must be a love that would compel one to sacrifice his/her life for another. This earthly love that we are seeking would have to be one that loves to the end of time without ceasing no matter what one does. This love would cause one to experience much pain and even tears at the disappointments of others and a feeling of great joy at the success of others. I have given much thought to this serious issue of love and have determined that there is only one earthly love that even comes close to meeting these very stringent guidelines. I think we can all agree that this very rare kind of earthly love can only be found in the case of a *"mother for her children"*. Let's ask another question that will help us better understand our initial question about God.

What does a mother want from her children?

She wants them to do well in life - to be prosperous.
She wants them to respect and be helpful to their siblings.
She wants them to be healthy, happy and wise.
She wants them to ask her for help only when they need it.
She wants them to be self-reliant and the best they can be.
She wants them to be honest and stay out of trouble.
She wants them to love her and remember Mother's Day.
She wants nothing for herself, seeing them happy is enough?

What does God want from us, His children?

I think God wants those same things from us that a mother wants. He wants, most of all, us to be prosperous and happy. For reference, you should read the "10 COMMANDMENTS" and there you'll find the full life strategy that God has laid out for us. Think for yourself!! Read for yourself!! My hope is that you will not allow people, who are no closer to God than you are, waste your time by strapping a lot of religious nonsense on your back for you to carry when you could be doing more important things that would truly please God; things like increasing the talents that he has given, things like becoming wealthy so that you can bless others, things like becoming a positive role model and thereby having others see your good works and glorify Him, the Father, which is in heaven. *To be clear, there is no love that compares to God's love for us.*

If you now believe that it's okay to be rich, and that God will be pleased with you, and He will celebrate your accomplishments with you, as the Master did with the first two servants in the ***Parable of The Talents***; then, you are now ready to learn and be blessed.

"Poverty and shame shall be to him that refuseth instruction".
(Prov. 13:18)

"I am the Lord thy God which teacheth thee to profit, which leadeth thee by the way that thou shouldest go". **(Isaiah 48:17)**

OUR INSTITUTIONS OF HIGHER LEARNING

<u>PRODUCING & TRAINING PROFESSIONAL SPENDERS AND BORROWERS</u>

Colleges and Universities, unfortunately, shy away from the **SUBJECT OF MONEY** and the **ACCUMULATION OF WEALTH.** This leaves a very severe void in students' learning and development process relative to money. This practice almost single-handedly renders our youth totally unprepared to survive or thrive in the very **SOPHISTICATED WORLD OF MONEY**. To be fair, these institutions do a fine job in preparing students with the knowledge they need in order to earn a great deal of money; but then, they send those same students away totally unprepared in regards to what to do with all that money they will earn. On the other hand, students are certainly taught the art of borrowing; you know, the student loan process at college enrollment and let's not forget those college campus-sponsored credit cards for the cafeteria, bookstore and other on-campus uses. By the time these students graduate, the colleges have helped to create a group of professional spenders and borrowers; which in most cases, have already amassed a serious amount of debt. Now at graduation, what do we have? We have a lot of 22 to 25-year old persons who only know how to spend and borrow.

In most instances, these college graduates have already amassed a $30,000 to $80,000 debt to pay-off even before they land their first job. To make matters even worse, they don't always get a job right away. Desperation begins to set in; but just in the nick-of-time, our young persons finally land a good paying job. The money is great! It's much more than they need to live on; however, all they have been taught to do is to *spend* & *borrow*. They go out and get more credit cards and charge each of them up to the credit limit; and then, they rent a fancy apartment and buy upscale furniture for it; and then, they buy a new luxury car. Can you see where this is going?

When students leave or graduate from most colleges and universities, they have been taught and prepared primarily to do these things; which are habits & lifestyles practiced by the poor and middle class:

(1) Spend and borrow money;
(2) Acquire multiple credit cards with high interest rates;
(3) Get a job and work for others;
(4) Earn a lot of money, and then spend it all as fast as it is earned;
(5) Become poor and middle class citizens; and
(6) Work until age 65, retire and die broke, end of story.

We would like to see colleges and universities starting to provide additional instruction and coursework, which place more conscious emphasis and deliberate awareness on preparing young people to adhere to these habits & lifestyles which are practiced by the rich and wealthy:

(1) Pay Themselves First;
(2) Pay Cash & Don't Borrow;
(3) Start their own businesses & have others work for them;
(4) Manage, Invest & Save money; making their money work for them;
(5) Become rich and powerful citizens; and
(6) Make a real difference in the world; and be a blessing to others.

ILL-PREPARING STUDENTS FOR THE SOPHISTICATED WORLD OF MONEY

Well, I guess these colleges and universities have left the task of teaching money smarts up to the parents. That's not a workable solution. Why, because most of these parents went to these same colleges and universities, and unfortunately have the same problems. They were also trained to be professional spenders and borrowers. And there you have it. There's no wonder why so many educated folks are making lots and lots of money and ending up broke after working all their lives. Is this intentional or is it just unawareness? I want to believe the latter, don't you?

Just for laughs, let's try to answer the question why is there such a shortcoming or deficiency in our institutions for higher learning as it pertains to educating our children about money and the management thereof. Speculation has it, that there are three fundamental reasons why Colleges and Universities shy away from offering extended courses having to do with the subject of money. Let's take a close look at each of them:

1. College and University administrators, professors, and executive staff members are, for the most part, POOR and MIDDLE CLASS people; therefore, they simply don't know much about money themselves. Remember, these people also went to these same colleges and universities that we just discussed, so they too, know much about borrowing and spending. These top educators are also ill-prepared and intimidated relative to the subject of money. It's nobody's fault, but it's still a problem that has created many financial cripples in the arena of money. The good news is, there's an easy fix.

2. Our society is one which benefits most from the
   working class. The working class consists of the
   poor and middle class among us; who tend to spend
   their money as fast as they earn it; which keeps the
   giant wheels of the economy turning in a desirable
   direction. If every one were rich, that could create a
   big problem. You see, the rich are rich because they
   do not spend all that they make as soon as they make
   it. They are rich because somewhere in their early
   development they learned to save rather than spend;
   they figured out the benefits of "paying themselves
   first" and how to make their money work for them.
   Furthermore, if we all were rich, who would work in
   the factories, on the farms, on the highway and by-
   ways; who would pick up the garbage; who would
   teach our children; who would work as policemen
   and protect us; who would work in our local super-
   markets and retail stores and etc? In other words,
   who would do all the things that the rich simply
   choose not to do. Why? Because these jobs don't
   pay enough money to make it worth their time. The
   rich are making so much money having others do
   their work for them; it just would not make good
   business sense for one who is rich to do these jobs.
   That having been said, it appears to be in the best

interest of our economy, our government and the rich to keep things just the way they are.

3. **O**ur system appears as though it is set-up so that **THE POOR GETS POORER** and **THE RICH GETS RICHER**. Since, the rich amongst us make all the laws and all the rules that govern us all, it's no wonder why IT IS THE WAY IT IS!

Can our institutions of higher learning fix this problem?

Sure they can! A much better and more appropriate question is, will they fix it now that we have created awareness? Only time will tell. In the meantime, where can one go to learn the honest truth and the facts about money? Common sense says that if you needed brain surgery, you would not go to a plumber or a lawyer; rather, you would go to a brain surgeon. Using that same logic and common sense, if one desires to become rich and wealthy; then, he/she needs to seek out and learn from those who are rich and wealthy.

THIS IS NOT ROCKET SCIENCE, IT'S JUST COMMON SENSE!

IMAGINE A WORLD WHERE YOU HAD THE POWER

Imagine a world where **"YOU"** had the power to create a new being as it were in the beginning. For reference, read the biblical story as told in the book of GENESIS 1:1; it starts thusly, "In the beginning GOD created the heaven and the earth". After GOD had created the earth and everything in it; then he created man. Man was the last of God's creations and perhaps justifiably appropriate. Thus, the creation of man was the finishing touch on this supreme, most majestic, and most magnificent work.

Why did God create man last? This question does make for some interesting debate and dialog. No one truly knows for sure why God selected to do it the way he did; however, there are many speculations relative to the topic. One thought is, since God's strategy was to create man in his own image with great mental intelligence that obviously would include the capacity to reason, plan and debate. God knew that creating man first could have caused him much undue, needless and unnecessary stress as man continues to instigate even until this day. Man may have gotten in God's way and might have delayed or altered this marvelous mission. So as to avoid needless drama and surely pointless debate, God created man last after all had been said and all had been done. Of course this is just one unverified theory of many. I'm sure that you have one theory that is just as possible.

The truth of the matter is, it really does not matter why man was created last. However, what does matter is that God must have favored and loved man, so much so, that he created him in his own GOD-like image. GENESIS 1:27 verifies this, "So God created man in his own image, in the image of God created he him; male and female created he them". Man was created with the **GOD-GIVEN** ability to accomplish anything that he **truly desires in his heart**. Even to this very day, after all the troubles man has caused and after all the mistakes man has made, God still shows favor and demonstrates great love towards him. God still allows man the exceptional ability to achieve things; almost anything, that he (man) can envision, he can achieve. Man needs only to truly believe and have an unwavering desire to achieve and so it is. God created man with the ability to move mountains; but first, man must think, believe and have faith that he can. Once the vision is clear, man must act on his vision with faith and belief and; thereby, develop a plan of action that will make his vision a reality. If he thinks he can, then he can. That's just the way it is; that's the way man was created by GOD.

FOR AS HE THINKETH IN HIS HEART, SO IS HE.   (Proverbs 23:7)

If a man is <u>POOR</u>, it's because he thinks poor and thereby does many of the things that lead to and produce the results of poverty;

and conversely,

If a man is <u>RICH</u>, it's because he thinks rich and thereby does many of the things that lead to and produce the results of wealth.

It's just that simple!   That's the way God created us. Incidentally, you don't have to imagine a world where YOU have the power to create a new being, as God did in the beginning, because we already live in such a world.   GOD has given each of us the unquestionable power to recreate **"A NEW BEING"** (ourselves) as often as we wish.   It's all in the mind; whatever you think is possible that is indeed what's possible.   And whatever you think is impossible, that indeed will be impossible for you.   IT IS WHAT IT IS; that's how we humans were created and there's nothing anyone can do to change that.   That's probably why man was created last so that he could not debate, question or change God's supreme creation plan.

Here's the ultimate deal, you can choose to be rich or you can choose to be poor or middle class. It's your decision completely and the world really doesn't care what you decide for yourself. However, your decision does impact all of those around you, your family, your loved ones, your children, your neighbors and etc. Every person who decides to and become financially successful is a light for others to see.

"LET YOUR LIGHT SO SHINE BEFORE MEN, THAT THEY MAY SEE YOUR GOOD WORKS, AND GLORIFY YOUR FATHER WHICH IS IN HEAVEN". (Matthew 5:15)

FOR AS HE THINKETH IN HIS HEART, SO IS HE. (Proverbs 23:7)

God has left this ultimate choice all up to each of us. You must choose wisely, my friends, and be blessed.

THREE MAJOR FACTS
TO REMEMBER ABOUT MONEY:

- *MONEY IS PLENTIFUL FOR THOSE WHO UNDERSTAND THE SIMPLE RULES AND SECRETS OF ITS ACQUISITION.*

- *IT MATTERS NOT HOW MUCH MONEY YOU MAKE; IT'S HOW MUCH MONEY YOU KEEP AND INVEST WISELY OF THAT WHICH YOU MAKE.*

- *MONEY IS THE ANSWER TO ALL THINGS.*

THE POOR THE MIDDLE CLASS AND THE RICH

Now that we've learned why society may have misinformed us on the principles & spiritual laws of money, let's do an exercise together to try and understand where you are in your circle of life. You see, there are only three groups/categories and everybody fits into one group or the other:

- ## THE POOR
- ## THE MIDDLE CLASS
- ## THE RICH

To help you more quickly and easily identify the group or category that best fits you, we will identify the most key and decisive habits & lifestyles; which will have the greatest impact relative to life status and financial growth or lack thereof. Once you get involved in this exercise, things will become clear and more comprehensible to you.

Are you ready?

Okay, let's go!

HABITS & LIFESTYLES

OF

THE POOR THE MIDDLE CLASS AND THE RICH

THE POOR

.......THEIR HABITS & LIFESTYLES.......

1. DON'T PAY THEMSELVES AT ALL

2. RENT THEIR DWELLING

3. WORK FOR MONEY (EMPLOYEES WORKING AN 8 TO 5 JOB)

4. NO DESIRE TO BE RICH (RELATES GODLINESS WITH POVERTY)

5. CREDIT CARDS - OVER THE LIMIT WITH HIGH INTEREST RATES

6. BUY NEITHER ASSETS NOR LIABILITIES (RENT MOST THINGS)

7. DON'T SEEK ADVICE - JUMP IN BLINDLY WITHOUT KNOWLEDGE

THE MIDDLE CLASS

........*THEIR HABITS & LIFESTYLES*..........

1. PAY THEMSELVES *LAST,* IF ANY MONEY IS LEFT OVER AFTER EXPENSES

2. BUY HOMES BEYOND THEIR FINANCIAL MEANS

3. WORK FOR MONEY *(EMPLOYEES WORKING AN 8 TO 5 JOB)*

4. HAVE A WHIMPY DESIRE TO BE RICH; NO REAL COMMITMENT

5. CREDIT CARDS - PAY MINIMUM MONTHLY CHARGES WITH NO END IN SIGHT

6. BUY LIABILITIES: *HOMES, BOATS, CARS, CLOTHES, JEWELRY & etc.*

7. TAKE ADVICE FROM FRIENDS, FAMILY & CHURCH FOLKS

8. TRY TO KEEP UP WITH THE JONESES *(BIG ISSUE WITH THE MIDDLE CLASS)*

THE RICH

.........*THEIR HABITS & LIFESTYLES*.............

1. PAY THEMSELVES *FIRST*

2. MAKE THEIR DWELLING A PROFITABLE INVESTMENT

3. MAKE THEIR MONEY WORK FOR THEM & HAVE OTHERS WORKING FOR THEM

4. HAVE AN UNWAVERING DESIRE TO BE RICH

5. PAY CASH & NEGOTIATE PRICING - *ONE CREDIT CARD FOR EMERGENCY USE*

6. BUY ASSETS: *INCOME PROPERTY, LAND, STOCKS, MUTUAL FUNDS & etc.*

7. SEEK ADVICE FROM OTHER COMPETENT & WEALTHY PEOPLE

Pay very close and special attention to the habits & life-styles of THE RICH.   Therein you will find the secrets for your starting focus. If you want to be rich, you must do the things that the rich people do. Otherwise, you will do the things that the POOR and the MIDDLE CLASS people do; which means, you will achieve the same results that they have achieved.

………NOT ROCKET SCIENCE, JUST COMMON SENSE………

Therefore, if you truly want to be rich, you must do what the rich folks do.   *NO EXCEPTIONS!!!*

Now, let's examine in detail each of the Habits & Lifestyles more closely. It is paramount that you learn the purpose and benefits behind each habit & lifestyle so that you can understand why it is so critical that you adhere to each and every one of them. This is not a hit and miss exercise. If you truly want wealth to find you, and if you want money to seek you out; then, you need only to follow the foot steps of those, like ourselves, who have achieved great wealth in this very same manner. It truly does work! **Let's Go!**

Upon initial investigation of these **HABITS & LIFESTYLES** of the **POOR** the **MIDDLE CLASS** & the **RICH;** if you are currently **POOR,** this exercise should help you to better understand **why?** You have been living the habits and lifestyles of the poor, haven't you? Aren't you tired of being poor? Of course you are. Here's the deal, "if you keep doing what you've been doing, you will keep getting what you've been getting", says Les Brown, a well known and renowned motivational speaker. Put another way, if you keep living the habits & lifestyles of the poor, you will remain poor.

NOT ROCKET SCIENCE, JUST COMMON SENSE!

STOP!!! Before we get involved with a more exhaustive examination and a more in-depth exploration of these exciting life changing and decisive HABITS & LIFESTYLES, let's deal with the first-thing-first – YOUR DEBT. Do You Have DEBT? If the answer is yes, you probably need help to terminate this DEBT before you can truly focus on this new and electrifying journey before you.

Your reading up to this point was intentionally organized and composed for the expressed purpose of:

> *Creating a positive mind-set that is receptive to change;*

> *Creating a belief that with God all things are possible and as one thinks, so is he;*

> *Persuading, relative to the notion, that money is good and the pursuit of it is noble and wise;*

> *Obtaining agreement that all of us should desire money and prosperity and to have a strong desire for money is perfectly okay and acceptable to God;*

> *Informing you that God wants us all to be rich and prosperous; He wants all of us to have life more abundantly; He rejoices in our good fortunes and encourages us to get up and try again when we fall.*

God wants you to be rich and prosperous and He is saying *"you can do it because I will help you, and all I need you to do is just believe in the life-changing task ahead"*. God understands debt, and we do to; so let's deal with that next.

PART TWO

GETTING-OUT-OF-DEBT

MR. DOWN & OUT

THE DEBT TERMINATOR

WHAT'S the BIG DEAL about DEBT?

Virtually, everyone has DEBT; so what's all the fuss about?

Here's the deal, if you're okay with being in debt and your indebtedness is not hurting you or those close to you; your current monthly income adequately supports your monthly debt obligations; then, there's no need for a whole lot of hullabaloo and worry. However, it's still wise to follow one of the debt termination options to keep your debt under control.

Now, on the other hand, if you are not okay with your current debt circumstances and your indebtedness is starting to hurt you as well as those close to you; then you need to seek wise counsel who can help you fix it as soon as you can. Here's how:

- *First, admit & acknowledge that you do have a debt problem;*

- *Second, have an objective & commitment to fix the problem;*

- *Third, understand that there is no shame in improving one's financial existence for the better; rather, there should be great pride and much satisfaction associated with the notion of personal self improvement; particularly, as it pertains to financial matters.*

Here are (4) very key and valuable lessons to learn before starting your new adventure towards debt free living & financial freedom.

1. *There is one sure way to create debt – SPENDING!*

2. *There's one sure way to accumulate wealth – SAVING!*

3. *You must CREATE A BUDGET to help discover and see where all the money is being spent. Since, it matters not how much money one earns, inherit or come into through some other means; it matters what you do with the money; how much of the money you keep of that which comes into your possession.*

4. *If it is to be, it is up to me; it ain't over until I win.*

TERMINATING DEBT

Unsecured debt is like a cancer. At first it is not life-threatening because it involves only a cell or two; but, it never stays small. It grows and grows until the patient can no longer endure the insurgence - then the patient dies. Without a plan or strategy to getting out of debt, reaching a goal of debt free living will remain a dream. However, a plan can turn a dream into a reality.

You may have tried to get-out-of-debt many times in the past, only to have your efforts end up in failure. To make matters even worst, you may have ended up in worst shape than when you started. Further, you have probably learned the hard way that not every debt counseling firm has your best interest at heart. We are familiar with and have heard horror stories where people have placed their trust in a debt-free counseling company and were taken total advantage of. We have spent many hours researching why this happens to good unsuspecting people and have concluded that when people are desperate they do desperate things. There are people who make a living preying on desperate people; just a friendly word of warning, buyers beware.

You'll need to be smart and very cautious when seeking help regarding your finances and your other key personal data. Seek advice and guidance from wise and competent people whom you trust; and people that have proven track-records dealing with matters of finance. Don't be afraid to ask for and check out their references. It's your life; it's your future; therefore, guard it as though your life depends on it, because it does. Remember, you don't want to get financial advice from someone who is in the process of filing personal bankruptcy. They can't even help themselves; and therefore, they surely can't help you. The very first step in the debt termination process is to admit and acknowledge that you have a serious DEBT problem as follows:

THE ADMISSION & ACKNOWLEDGMENT: I am a SPENDER!!!

"I AM A SPENDER!!! AND THAT'S NOT AT ALL GOOD FOR ME".

"I AM A SPENDER!!! AND THAT'S WHY I AM NOT FINANCIALLY FREE".

"I AM A SPENDER!!! AND THAT'S WHY I HAVE NO POWER & INFLUENCE".

"I AM A SPENDER!!! AND THAT'S WHY MY LIFE IS NOT FULL OF JOY".

"I AM A SPENDER!!! AND THAT'S WHY I HAVE LOW SELF-ESTEEM".

"I AM A SPENDER!!! AND THAT'S WHY I AM ALWAYS SO AFRAID".

"I AM A SPENDER!!! AND THAT'S WHY I AM IN SO MUCH DEBT".

"I AM A SPENDER!!! AND THAT'S WHY MY FAMILY IS AT RISK".

"I AM A SPENDER!!! AND THAT'S WHY I HAVE NO MONEY".

"I AM A SPENDER!!! AND THAT'S WHY I NEED HELP NOW".

Then, follow with an objective and commitment statement that sets the goal to be achieved:

THE OBJECTIVE & COMMITMENT: *I will become a saver!!!*

"To achieve my dreams, I must cease to be a spender, and do everything in my power to become a SAVER!!!   I know that becoming <u>a SAVER is intelligent and wise,</u> and the only sure way of accumulating wealth and riches. I need all the help that I can get and I promise that I will do whatever it takes to resolve my indebtedness and spending problem".

Here are *(4) PROVEN OPTIONS* which can help you *GET-OUT-OF-DEBT.* You should choose the option or approach that you feel most comfortable with and the one that best fits your unique situation. While we believe it is possible for most people to make an acceptable choice on their own, don't be afraid or overly embarrassed to at least talk to an expert in these matters, i.e. debt free counselor or some other debt professionals. Remember, some Debt Free counseling groups are more concerned about the money they can make as a result of your distressed and unfortunate circumstance, rather than what is really best for you. Therefore, you must take great care in choosing one who will work best with you, and who will put your needs and concerns before their motivation to make money. The first and most important step in this debt elimination process is to **_CREATE A BUDGET_** **(A FINANCIAL SNAPSHOT)** which will help you better understand exactly where you are, financially. It will also help you to determine which option will most likely play well in your circumstance. It is imperative that this **BUDGET PLANNING DOCUMENT** is prepared thoroughly and honestly. Be truthful and don't kid yourself; for if you do, you will make matters even more stressful for yourself and your family. *This budget is your financial life on paper!! Take it seriously and spend the time that is required to do it right.*

Let's take a closer look at these four (4) options and approaches for getting you out of debt.

4 PROVEN OPTIONS FOR GETTING-OUT-OF-DEBT

1. EARN MORE MONEY - CREATE MORE INCOME

- CREATE A BUDGET PLAN & ADHERE TO IT WITHOUT DEVIATION
- GET A SECOND JOB & ASK YOUR BOSS FOR A RAISE
- START YOUR OWN BUSINESS
- IMPROVE YOUR CURRENT SKILLS OR LEARN A NEW SKILL
- BUY RENTAL PROPERTY *(BUY A DUPLEX, MOVE IN, LIVE RENT-FREE; LET THE TENANT PAY YOUR MORTGAGE PAYMENT AND PUT CASH IN YOUR POCKET)*

2. CHANGE SPENDING HABITS - CONTROL EXPENDITURES

- CREATE A BUDGET PLAN & ADHERE TO IT WITHOUT DEVIATION
- THINK SAVE; RATHER THAN SPEND
- LET EVERYTHING YOU DO BE MONEY DRIVEN
- BUY ASSETS & MAKE YOUR MONEY WORK FOR YOU
- SHOP FOR BARGAINS *(BUY IN BULK, i.e. SAM'S CLUB, ETC)*
- PAY CASH - CUT UP ALL CREDIT CARDS EXCEPT ONE FOR EMERGENCIES
- PAY YOURSELF FIRST A MINIMUM OF 10% OF ALL EARNINGS *(BECOME YOUR OWN BANKER; BORROW FROM YOURSELF; PAY YOURSELF HIGH INTEREST RATES)*

3. FILE BANKRUPTCY - GET A FRESH NEW START!!!

- CREATE A BUDGET PLAN TO DETERMINE IF BANKRUPTCY IS THE RIGHT THING
- IF MONTHLY EXPENSES ARE FAR GREATER THAN YOUR MONTHLY INCOME
- IF YOUR DEBT IS IMPOSSIBLE TO PAY-OFF (LOST JOB/PROLONGED ILLNESS)
- IF EVERYTHING ELSE HAS FAILED AND THERE IS NO OTHER WAY OUT

4. MARRY A RICH PERSON - ONE WHO CAN HELP PAY-OFF YOUR DEBT

RESOLUTION OF DEBT

The sooner you can become free of all debt, the sooner you can begin to accumulate wealth; which is, or should be, the main focus and primary purpose of this undertaking. Let's take a closer and more in-depth look at the four (4) OPTIONS that have just been identified for the expressed purpose of terminating debt.

EARN MORE MONEY OR CREATE MORE INCOME

Creating more income can help you pay off your debt much faster and that's a good thing. Let's look at some ways to make more money available.

GET A SECOND JOB and ASKING YOUR BOSS FOR A RAISE are the two great ideas which can be implemented without much preparation or cash investment on your part. These can be put in affect almost immediately. It makes good business to institute one or both of these as soon as possible, the-sooner-the-better; since, they will provide and create almost instantaneous relief in a desperate-for-cash situation. STARTING A BUSINESS, SKILLS UPGRADES and PURCHASING RENTAL PROPERTY will require considerable time on your part as well as some cash outlay, which you probably will not have right away. These should be long term strategies which would be best put-into-play over time as you continued to work a second job. STARTING A BUSINESS and PURCHASING RENTAL PROPERTY (a duplex would represent the least cash outlay and the easiest venture for the first-timer) are two very exciting strategies that can help one pay-off debt and provide a tremendous low-risk opportunity for accumulating significant wealth in the future. Also, be aware that while these two ventures are assets and can help you create wealth; they will initially create even more debt for you. However, we consider buying assets, such as a DUPLEX, to be "good debt"; which is an investment in your future and the future of your children, if you will. The duplex rental income property is a sound investment which will allow its owner the opportunity to live in it for free; while his tenant pays the monthly mortgage. We'll talk more about the "DUPLEX" RENTAL INCOME PROPERTY later in the Habits & Lifestyles of the Rich. *You will also discover that most rich people own their own businesses.*

CHANGE SPENDING HABITS & CONTROL EXPENDITURES

Changing spending habits and controlling your expenditures can increase the amount of monthly cash availability that you can put towards paying off your debt more quickly. This option looks at the notion of stretching your money, so to speak. In other words, we explore ways to make a dollar buy more, and we learn to think about saving a dollar; rather than spending it. We learn to watch and manage each of our dollars every day; making sure that we are getting the most bang for our bucks.

The major difference between a rich person and a poor person is their spending habits and the financial decisions they make regarding their money. Rich folks have a definite strategy for their lives and a well thought-out budget plan for their money. Rich folks seriously do not like spending money, they get more satisfaction out of making it grow and accumulate. While on the other hand, poor folks can't wait for payday so that they can get their paycheck and promptly go out and spend every dime of it. Then comes next week and they do it all over again. In fact, most poor folks will have spent most of their paycheck money before they get it. You've heard poor people say, "I can't wait to get paid so that I can buy that _____ " (you fill in the blank.) And that is the simple and truthful reason why these people are poor; there's no mystery here, just a tragic tale of an "old poor man" who walks around amazed at how he could've possibly worked all his life and accumulated nothing. What a pity. What a shame. What an awful tragedy that could have easily been avoided simply by **CHANGING HIS SPENDING HABITS**. Don't let this happen to you!! Don't let this happen to your family! It's a fate that is almost worst than death.

It's a simple decision. If you want to be rich, you must save and invest wisely in assets; and when you do spend, pay cash and get the most out of your dollars. Possibly the most key spending practice or rule that the rich adhere to is paying themselves first before they pay anyone else. I need not tell you how to be poor, most of you already know that process all too well. And if you want to keep getting the same results just keep doing the same things that you've been doing. Your decision to get out of debt and become more financially secure can be an easy one; since we have developed this simple "how to" road map which makes it a no-brainer" to get where you want to go financially. Choose an option that gets you out of debt quickly; then start practicing the habits & lifestyles of the rich. It has all been laid out for you in the next chapter.........

"Habits & Lifestyles - an in-depth comparison".

FILE BANKRUPTCY - GET A FRESH NEW START!!!

In very serious and complicated indebtedness situations where it is all but impossible to make the ends meet and neither of the first two or the fourth options can produce any significant relief or results, it may be necessary and advisable for one to __file bankruptcy__.   Bankruptcy provides a new and fresh start for those who have no other way out. Bankruptcy was once thought of as one of the most disgusting, disgraceful and most distasteful acts in society's social setting.   Not so today, with the ever changing world economy, failing and declining job markets, sometimes this is the only way to re-create your life.

The primary reasons for filing bankruptcy for individuals are unforeseen loss of employment, excessive credit card debt, medical expenses and divorce.   Needless to say, many of these situations create both financial difficulty as well as cause a tremendous amount of disruption and stress in and of themselves.   Thus, it is especially important that individuals consider all available options and bankruptcy alternatives to make sure whatever action they choose to pursue is in their long-term best interest.

There are two main chapters of personal bankruptcy under which individuals can file: **CHAPTER 7** and **CHAPTER 13**. **CHAPTER 7 BANKRUPTCY** is a liquidation of assets; while **CHAPTER 13 BANKRUPTCY** is reorganization where the debtor creates a three to five year payment plan. If one determines that bankruptcy is the best option available then one should consult with an attorney with experience in the personal bankruptcy field. Do not use a beginner here. Don't let a new inexperienced lawyer train himself on your case; you may be sorry, if you do. Don't try to do it yourself to save money; that's just plain foolish, unless you are a lawyer. However, if you are a lawyer and find yourself having to file bankruptcy; then, it may be a good idea for you to get a good lawyer as well.

Remember, one of the primary goals of the bankruptcy laws are to provide DEBTORS WITH FINANCIAL DIFFICULTY AN OPPORTUNITY FOR A FRESH AND NEW START. Therefore, choose wisely and be smart when you opt for bankruptcy. Chapter 7 bankruptcy pretty much sets you free; while Chapter 13 provides you medication to ease the pain. When you file bankruptcy, whether Chapter 7 or Chapter 13, the credit implications are similar; therefore, you should probably consider Chapter 7 if at all possible. It's your responsibility to convince and help your attorney create an agreeable Chapter 7 Bankruptcy filing document package for approval by the courts.

MARRY A RICH PERSON - ONE WHO CAN PAY-OFF YOUR DEBT

Marrying the right person who can satisfy all of ones needs; whether those needs are financial, emotional or otherwise, has always been the hallmark for marital unions since the beginning of time. If given a choice, any wise person would marry someone who can provide essential and critical assistance relative to their specific lifestyle requirements; be they financial or otherwise.

I can see nothing inherently wrong with anyone marrying for better; nor can I see anything flawed with the notion of one making a conscious and informed financial decision when choosing a mate.

A MAJOR WARNING REGARDING DEBT QUICK FIXES!!

When achieving debt-free status through a bankruptcy or through a marriage where the debt is paid-off by another party other than the one who created the debt; unfortunately, no lessons relative to appropriate financial dealings were learned. Therefore, it is highly probable that our new debt free friend will soon be back in debt again if they are not indeed careful. Why? Because by taking these two quick and easy ways out, one did not practice or learn the behaviors necessary for practical and sound financial health. Utilizing options 1 & 2; one gains an invaluable experience that will prove to be a tremendous financial benefit and advantage for years to come. These two options represent the idea or notion of doing it the hard way; the old fashion way or even best said, the Smith Barney way, THEY EARN IT. Whichever way one chooses to get-out-of-debt, let me assure you that it's okay, just do it.

All that having been said, go for it. Miss Donna and I wish you and yours a good and prosperous life; filled with much joy and financial abundance.

Be very careful to remember what you went through because I don't think you desire to repeat the "DEBT" ordeal again. Do you want to go through that painful existence again? Do you remember how embarrassing it was to face your family and how hard it was to keep it a secret from your friends? Can you remember how frustrating and difficult it was trying to keep up your image and appearances near the end when things started to fall apart? You remember, it was pure hell, wasn't it? You know that Debt can destroy families; you may not be so lucky next time. Be smart; don't end up like *"MR. DOWN & OUT"* below. There's a song that I like very much and it was made popular in the 60's by my all-time favorite singer, ***Mr. Sam Cooke***, it goes simply; ***"Nobody wants you when you're down and out; because, if in your pocket you have not one penny, you look around for all them good friends that you thought you had and you find out that you don't have any. I want to tell you about it and about it I have no doubt that nobody wants you, nobody needs you, nobody wants you when you're down and out".***

"MR. DOWN & OUT"

Let's recap the problem one more time for affect; just a little reminder, so that you will not easily forget. What's the first thing one in serious debt must do in order for him/her and THE DEBT TERMINATOR to be successful? Let's go, you know the drill.

One must first admit and acknowledge that he/she has a serious DEBT problem!!!

THE ADMISSION & ACKNOWLEDGMENT: *I am a SPENDER!!!*

"I AM A SPENDER!!! AND THAT'S NOT AT ALL GOOD FOR ME".

"I AM A SPENDER!!! AND THAT'S WHY I AM NOT FINANCIALLY FREE".

"I AM A SPENDER!!! AND THAT'S WHY I HAVE NO POWER & INFLUENCE".

"I AM A SPENDER!!! AND THAT'S WHY MY LIFE IS NOT FULL OF JOY".

"I AM A SPENDER!!! AND THAT'S WHY I HAVE LOW SELF-ESTEEM".

"I AM A SPENDER!!! AND THAT'S WHY I AM ALWAYS SO AFRAID".

"I AM A SPENDER!!! AND THAT'S WHY I AM IN SO MUCH DEBT".

"I AM A SPENDER!!! AND THAT'S WHY MY FAMILY IS AT RISK".

"I AM A SPENDER!!! AND THAT'S WHY I HAVE NO MONEY".

"I AM A SPENDER!!! AND THAT'S WHY I NEED HELP NOW".

Then, follow with an objective and commitment statement that sets the goal to be achieved:

THE OBJECTIVE & COMMITMENT: _I will become a SAVER!!!_

"To achieve my dreams, I must cease to be a spender, and do everything in my power to become a SAVER!!! I know that to become <u>a SAVER is intelligent and wise,</u> and the only sure way of accumulating wealth and riches. I need all the help that I can get and I promise that I will do whatever it takes to resolve my indebtedness and spending problem".

Now that we have concluded this very depressing and dismal task which dealt with you getting-out-of-debt, let's get on to the more exciting and electrifying mission of teaching you "How to" become "Rich and Wealthy" beyond your wildest dreams!!!!!!!!!!!!

PART THREE

ACCUMULATING WEALTH

THREE FUNDAMENTAL REQUIREMENTS
FOR
ACHIEVING WEALTH:

---

1. **DEVELOP A POSITIVE MENTAL ATTITUDE TOWARD MONEY, PROSPERITY AND FINANCIAL RESPONSIBILITY; WITH AN UNWAVERING DESIRE TO BE RICH.**

2. **DEVELOP A PRACTICAL & EFFECTIVE STRATEGY TO MAXIMIZE YOUR GOD GIVEN POWER TO CREATE WEALTH & FINANCIAL INDEPENDENCE.**

3. **LEARN AND ADHERE TO EACH OF THE HABITS AND LIFESTYLES PRACTICED BY THE RICH AS DESCRIBED IN THIS BOOK.**

NO EXCEPTIONS!!!!!!!!!

HABITS & LIFESTYLES
- AN INDEPTH COMPARISON

With your agreement, we are about to begin a journey that will educate you, inspire you and hopefully change your financial position and future for the better. More importantly, this exercise will provide you, for the first time, a simple and easy to understand approach to achieving FINANCIAL INDEPENDENCE and security for yourself and your family. Remember, if you want to be rich you must do what the rich people do - no exceptions. If you're not serious about improving your financial future, don't waste your time with this exercise or this book. You should give this book as a gift to someone who you care about and who you want to see do well financially. If you are on-board and determine to be rich and wealthy, let's look at the first and most crucial of all the HABITS AND LIFESTYLES –

"PAY YOURSELF FIRST"

PAYING YOURSELF FIRST is the most crucial of all the habits & lifestyles. According to the U.S. Census Bureau, Census 2000 Summary, 77.5% of all working people in America earned less than $75,000/year which include the Poor and Middle Class in our society. 35% of all Americans earned $29,999 per year or less; and just 12.7% earned $100,000 per year or more. About 65% (U.S. Census Bureau, Census 2000 Summary) of all working people in America earn $30,000.00 or more per year and well over $1 Million in a 30-year work career. What's so disturbing and pathetic is the fact that many of these same Americans end up broke after earning over $1 Million dollars in their life time. Even more unbelievable, the total earnings in most of these households could add up to over **$2 MILLION** when the equivalent earnings of spouses are taken into consideration. In American homes, with two people working and earning over $2 million dollars in their 30-year work careers, it is absolutely ludicrous and absurd for this much money to just vanish without a trace. How could this vanishing act possibly happen to so many wise and intelligent people? Where and how could $2,000,000.00 disappear? Something must have gone terribly wrong. Let's explore some of the possibilities.

These folks probably did <u>not</u> pay themselves first. They most likely spent all their money as fast as they earned it on things that were mostly rented.   My guess would be that they perhaps lived those habits & lifestyles practiced by the POOR and the Middle Class.   At this time it may be a good idea to take a few minutes to go back and review the habits & lifestyles of the three groups side by side.   Once you have refreshed your memory regarding all three habits & lifestyles, you will be more equipped to better understand and grasp the following concepts:

Notice the first and most <u>fatal</u> habit & lifestyle of the POOR:

<u>"DON'T PAY THEMSELVES AT ALL"</u>

The POOR spend their money as fast as they earn it on things that are mostly rented. Which means there will be no residual or appreciated values accrued; thus we see, everything is gone with nothing left to show for all that money spent in their life times.

Now, notice the first and also most fatal habit & lifestyle of the MIDDLE CLASS:

"PAY THEMSELVES LAST, IF ANY MONEY IS LEFT OVER AFTER EXPENSES"

The Middle Class do **not** pay themselves first either. In fact, they pay themselves last if any money is left over after all the bills have been paid. In most of these hit and miss situations, where there is no **BUDGET PLANNING or SPENDING DISCIPLINE**, there is usually very little or no money left over. Much like the POOR, the Middle Class also spends their money just as fast as they earn it on things that are mostly classified as **"LIABILITIES"**. **Liabilities** are purchases such as clothing, cars, boats, jewelry and even a personal home that is not paid off in full. One way to determine whether an item or product is a Liability is to ask the question: if I lose my job, will this item be a source of regular income? If the answer is no; then, there is a very good probability that the item or product is a **LIABILITY. ASSETS** are the opposite of **LIABILITIES,** they will provide regular income whether the owner's job is lost or not.

The **POOR** as well as the **MIDDLE CLASS** will end up BROKE after a 30-year working career. Why? It is simply because they make the fatal mistake of not paying themselves first every time they get paid.

The POOR and the MIDDLE CLASS never build up any substantial cash reserves; and therefore, the smallest family emergency or unanticipated expenditure causes great anxiety and creates additional expenses which causes other bad habits to form - Credit card spending – robbing Peter to pay Paul; debt on top of debt and before long it's out of control. At this point, financial independence and security can be kissed good-bye.   Where did all that money go?   *Credit cards* with high interest rates; *no assets* to produce added income; *no cash reserves* to eliminate borrowing; these are all the results of not paying themselves first.   These folks (the POOR and the Middle Class) will end up broke after working and making good money for 30 years and more. What a pity. What a shame. How incredibly stupid one must be to live life that way?

Finally, let's learn and adhere to the first most decisive and most fundamental habit & lifestyle practiced by the RICH:

"PAY THEMSELVES FIRST"

The Rich pay themselves first a minimum of 10% of their gross income - **NO EXCEPTIONS!** Strict adherence to the Pay Yourself First financial strategy will create a tremendous **CASH RESERVE** in a very short period of time. Take a look at Exhibit 2: Earning $30,000 thousand dollars per year each; paying themselves first a minimum of 10%; and accruing at a minimum interest rate of only 5%, a couple accumulates over $6,000 the first year; over $28,000 by the fourth year; almost $54,000 by the seventh year and over $82,000 by year ten. The Pay Yourself First plan creates a significant and continuously growing cash reserves that will, in essence, allow one to become his/her own **Banker**; and thereby providing themselves and their family these benefits:

- **MONEY!** Knowing that you have it; oh what a great feeling.
- Guaranteed achievement of **FINANCIAL INDEPENDENCE & SECURITY**
- Cash reserves readily available for **FAMILY EMERGENCIES**
- Cash reserves that can be used for financing **COLLEGE EDUCATIONS**
- Cash reserves that **ELIMINATE BORROWING** at the bank's high interest rates
- Cash reserves allowing access to wise **LUCRATIVE & SAFE INVESTMENTS**
- Cash reserves providing a **FINANCIAL SAFETY NET** for retirement
- **MONEY WORKING 24 HOURS PER DAY** making more money for its owner.

You must admit that this is an absolutely fantastic strategy and anyone can follow it. Now hold on a minute, before you get too carried away and excited about all those cash reserves that you will created via the **PAY YOURSELF FIRST** plan, let's review the rules and regulations deployed by the RICH to govern usage of the Pay Yourself First cash reserve funds:

RULES & REGULATIONS GOVERNING USAGE OF CASH RESERVE FUNDS:

1. *All funds used are considered a LOAN; which must be repaid with interest equal to the current interest rates that would have been charged if this loan had been secured through a banking institution; or at the 10% assumed investment return rate, whichever is greater.*

2. *While LOAN is being repaid, there can be no interruption in the 10% minimum Pay Yourself First plan - NO EXCEPTIONS!*

3. *A promissory note which guarantees PAYMENT-IN-FULL must be notarized, signed by all participants, and filed in safe deposit box or fire-proof safe.*

Let's look at three couples who earned $30,000 each per year, totaling $60,000 per year for each couple. Now, let's assume that they all invested their "Pay Yourself First" savings in a Bank Money Market Fund or a Mutual Fund that yielded an annual return on investment (ROI) of 10%. In this scenario, we want to demonstrate how tremendously rewarding the **"PAY YOURSELF FIRST"** plan can be for those people who are willing to stretch beyond the 10% minimum. Take a look at these incredible 30 year "Pay Yourself First" results:

> *Couple "A" paying themselves a minimum of __10% of their gross earnings__ over a 30-year period or $500/month; giving this result: Principle + Interest (30 yrs.) = $1,183,756.*

> *Couple "B" paying themselves a total of __15% of their gross earnings__ over a 30-year period or $750/month; giving this result: Principle + Interest (30 yrs.) = $1,775.635.*

> *Couple "C" paying themselves a total of __20% of their gross earnings__ over a 30-year period or $1,000/month; giving this result: Principle + Interest (30 yrs.) = $2,367,513.*

It is so painfully obvious that there are major and overwhelming benefits derived from this first *HABIT & LIFESTYLE PRACTICE BY THE RICH* - **PAY YOURSELF FIRST.** There is truly no logical reason why anyone who works and earns good money for thirty years should end up broke. However, you know what they say, "a fool and his money will soon part".

I have included Exhibits (2 thru 5) to further illustrate the **PAY YOURSELF FIRST – 30 YEAR INVESTMENT EARNINGS ANALYSIS PLAN.** Exhibit 6 is a blank budget sheet that you can use to begin your own personal budget analysis plan. **See exhibits on pages that follow:**

(EXHIBIT 2) - Couple earning $30,000 each, totaling $60,000/yr.
(EXHIBIT 3) - Couple earning $50,000 each, totaling $100,000/yr.
(EXHIBIT 4) - Couple earning $75,000 each, totaling $150,000/yr.
(EXHIBIT 5) - One earning $80,000 & one @$100,000 totaling $180,000/yr.
(EXHIBIT 6) - A Manual Budgeting Form for your personal budget planning.

These **EXHIBITS** give an exciting and accurate account of what "could be" achieved if one would but follow the simple and straight-forward first habit & lifestyle practiced by the RICH; whereas they PAY THEMSELVES FIRST no less than ten percent of the gross income that they earn. Adherence to this one habit & lifestyle alone will create financial independence and security that could eliminate many stresses associated with growing old. It creates an almost instant cash reserve that will allow you to borrow from yourself; whereas, you earn the interest dollars rather than paying them to a bank; thus, making your money work even harder for you. Additionally, it guarantees a safe and comfortable retirement plan for anyone who earns a good income for a prolonged work career. IT'S NOT ROCKET SCIENCE, IT'S JUST COMMON SENSE!!!!!

EXHIBITS

#2 PAY YOURSELF FIRST - 30 YEAR ANALYSIS (A COUPLE EARNING $60,000/YR.)

#3 PAY YOURSELF FIRST - 30 YEAR ANALYSIS (A COUPLE EARNING $100,000/YR.)

#4 PAY YOURSELF FIRST - 30 YEAR ANALYSIS (A COUPLE EARNING $150,000/YR.)

#5 PAY YOURSELF FIRST - 30 YEAR ANALYSIS (A COUPLE EARNING $180,000/YR.)

#6 PAY YOURSELF FIRST - **MANUAL BUDGET PLANNING FORM FOR YOUR PERSONAL INPUT**

(SEE NEXT FIVE SHEETS OF EXHIBITS)

PAY YOURSELF FIRST

30 YEAR INVESTMENT EARNINGS ANALYSIS

ITEMS of CONSIDERATION	ANNUAL INCOME	MTHLY. INCOME	MONTHLY SAVINGS 1st DUPLEX PURCHASE	PAY YOURSELF FIRST PLAN @10%	PAY YOURSELF FIRST PLAN @20%
WIFE	30,000.00		0.00	0.00	0.00
HUSBAND	30,000.00		0.00	0.00	0.00
Tithes & God's Work @10%			0.00	500.00	500.00
Pay Yourself First @10 & 20%			0.00	**500.00**	**1,000.00**
Live Rent-Free in Duplex - Savings			500.00	*0.00*	*0.00*
Auto Payment & Expenses			0.00	0.00	0.00
Medical & Life Insurances			0.00	0.00	0.00
Entertainment/Clothing, etc.			0.00	0.00	0.00
Credit Card Payments			0.00	0.00	0.00
TOTALS	$ 60,000.00	$ -	$ 500.00	$ 1,000.00	$ 1,500.00

			Savings Accrued From Free Rental in Duplex	Pay Yourself First PLAN @10%	Pay Yourself First PLAN @20%
Pay Yourself First Cash Invested Each Month			$ 500.00	$ 500.00	$ 1,000.00
	Plus interest @5%				
ACCRUED Cash 1 Year	5.00		6,300.00	6,300.00	12,600.00
ACCRUED Cash 2 Years	5.00		13,230.00	13,230.00	26,460.00
ACCRUED Cash 3 Years	5.00		20,506.50	20,506.50	41,013.00
ACCRUED Cash 4 Years	5.00		28,146.83	28,146.83	56,293.65
ACCRUED Cash 5 Years	5.00		36,169.17	36,169.17	72,338.33
ACCRUED Cash 6 Years	5.00		44,592.62	44,592.62	89,185.25
ACCRUED Cash 7 Years	5.00		53,437.26	53,437.26	106,874.51
ACCRUED Cash 8 Years	5.00		62,724.12	62,724.12	125,448.24
ACCRUED Cash 9 Years	5.00		72,475.32	72,475.32	144,950.65
ACCRUED Cash 10 Years	5.00		82,714.09	82,714.09	165,428.18
ACCRUED Cash 11 Years	5.00		93,464.80	93,464.80	186,929.59
ACCRUED Cash 12 Years	5.00		104,753.04	104,753.04	209,506.07
ACCRUED Cash 13 Years	5.00		116,605.69	116,605.69	233,211.37
ACCRUED Cash 14 Years	5.00		129,050.97	129,050.97	258,101.94
ACCRUED Cash 15 Years	5.00		142,118.52	142,118.52	284,237.04
ACCRUED Cash 16 Years	5.00		155,839.45	155,839.45	311,678.89
ACCRUED Cash 17 Years	5.00		170,246.42	170,246.42	340,492.84
ACCRUED Cash 18 Years	5.00		185,373.74	185,373.74	370,747.48
ACCRUED Cash 19 Years	5.00		201,257.43	201,257.43	402,514.85
ACCRUED Cash 20 Years	5.00		217,935.30	217,935.30	435,870.59
ACCRUED Cash 21 Years	5.00		235,447.06	235,447.06	470,894.12
ACCRUED Cash 22 Years	5.00		253,834.42	253,834.42	507,668.83
ACCRUED Cash 23 Years	5.00		273,141.14	273,141.14	546,282.27
ACCRUED Cash 24 Years	5.00		293,413.19	293,413.19	586,826.39
ACCRUED Cash 25 Years	5.00		314,698.85	314,698.85	629,397.70
ACCRUED Cash 26 Years	5.00		337,048.79	337,048.79	674,097.59
ACCRUED Cash 27 Years	5.00		360,516.23	360,516.23	721,032.47
ACCRUED Cash 28 Years	5.00		385,157.05	385,157.05	770,314.09
ACCRUED Cash 29 Years	5.00		411,029.90	411,029.90	822,059.80
ACCRUED Cash 30 Years	5.00		$ 438,196.39	$ 438,196.39	$ 876,392.79

				10%	20%
			WIFE	$250.00	$500.00
			HUSBAND	$250.00	$500.00

EXHIBIT 2

PAY YOURSELF FIRST

30 YEAR INVESTMENT EARNINGS ANALYSIS

ITEMS of CONSIDERATION	ANNUAL INCOME	MTHLY. INCOME	MONTHLY SAVINGS 1st DUPLEX PURCHASE	PAY YOURSELF FIRST PLAN @10%	PAY YOURSELF FIRST PLAN @20%
WIFE	50,000.00		0.00	0.00	0.00
HUSBAND	50,000.00		0.00	0.00	0.00
Tithes & God's Work @10%			0.00	833.33	833.33
Pay Yourself First @10 & 20%			0.00	833.33	1,666.67
Living Rent Free Mortgage			600.00	0.00	0.00
Auto Payment & Expenses			0.00	0.00	0.00
Medical & Life Insurances			0.00	0.00	0.00
Entertainment/Clothing, etc.			0.00	0.00	0.00
Credit Card Payments			0.00	0.00	0.00
TOTALS	$ 100,000.00	$ -	$ 600.00	$ 1,666.67	$ 2,500.00

			Savings Accrued From Free Rental In Duplex	Pay Yourself First PLAN @10%	Pay Yourself First PLAN @20%
Pay Yourself First Cash Invested Each Month			$ 600.00	$ 833.33	$ 1,666.67
	Plus interest @10%				
ACCRUED Cash 1 Year	10.00		7,920.00	11,000.00	22,000.00
ACCRUED Cash 2 Years	10.00		17,424.00	24,200.00	48,400.00
ACCRUED Cash 3 Years	10.00		27,878.40	38,720.00	77,440.00
ACCRUED Cash 4 Years	10.00		39,378.24	54,692.00	109,384.00
ACCRUED Cash 5 Years	10.00		52,028.06	72,261.20	144,522.40
ACCRUED Cash 6 Years	10.00		65,942.87	91,587.32	183,174.64
ACCRUED Cash 7 Years	10.00		81,249.16	112,846.05	225,692.10
ACCRUED Cash 8 Years	10.00		98,086.07	136,230.66	272,461.31
ACCRUED Cash 9 Years	10.00		116,606.68	161,953.72	323,907.45
ACCRUED Cash 10 Years	10.00		136,979.35	190,249.10	380,498.19
ACCRUED Cash 11 Years	10.00		159,389.28	221,374.00	442,748.01
ACCRUED Cash 12 Years	10.00		184,040.21	255,611.41	511,222.81
ACCRUED Cash 13 Years	10.00		211,156.23	293,272.55	586,545.09
ACCRUED Cash 14 Years	10.00		240,983.86	334,699.80	669,399.60
ACCRUED Cash 15 Years	10.00		273,794.24	380,269.78	760,539.56
ACCRUED Cash 16 Years	10.00		309,885.67	430,396.76	860,793.52
ACCRUED Cash 17 Years	10.00		349,586.23	485,536.43	971,072.87
ACCRUED Cash 18 Years	10.00		393,256.86	546,190.08	1,092,380.16
ACCRUED Cash 19 Years	10.00		441,294.54	612,909.09	1,225,818.17
ACCRUED Cash 20 Years	10.00		494,136.00	686,299.99	1,372,599.99
ACCRUED Cash 21 Years	10.00		552,261.60	767,029.99	1,534,059.99
ACCRUED Cash 22 Years	10.00		616,199.75	855,832.99	1,711,665.99
ACCRUED Cash 23 Years	10.00		686,531.73	953,516.29	1,907,032.58
ACCRUED Cash 24 Years	10.00		763,896.90	1,060,967.92	2,121,935.84
ACCRUED Cash 25 Years	10.00		848,998.59	1,179,164.71	2,358,329.43
ACCRUED Cash 26 Years	10.00		942,610.45	1,309,181.18	2,618,362.37
ACCRUED Cash 27 Years	10.00		1,045,583.50	1,452,199.30	2,904,398.61
ACCRUED Cash 28 Years	10.00		1,158,853.85	1,609,519.23	3,219,038.47
ACCRUED Cash 29 Years	10.00		1,283,451.23	1,782,571.16	3,565,142.31
ACCRUED Cash 30 Years	10.00		$ 1,420,508.36	$ 1,972,928.27	$ 3,945,856.54
				10%	20%
			WIFE	$416.67	$833.33
			HUSBAND	$416.67	$833.33

EXHIBIT 3

PAY YOURSELF FIRST

30 YEAR INVESTMENT EARNINGS ANALYSIS

ITEMS of CONSIDERATION	ANNUAL INCOME	MTHLY. INCOME	MONTHLY SAVINGS 1st DUPLEX PURCHASE	PAY YOURSELF FIRST PLAN @10%	PAY YOURSELF FIRST PLAN @20%
WIFE	75,000.00		0.00	0.00	0.00
HUSBAND	75,000.00		0.00	0.00	0.00
Tithes & God's Work @10%			0.00	1,250.00	1,250.00
Pay Yourself First @10 & 20%			0.00	1,250.00	2,500.00
Living Rent Free Mortgage			750.00	0.00	0.00
Auto Payment & Expenses			0.00	0.00	0.00
Medical & Life Insurances			0.00	0.00	0.00
Entertainment/Clothing, etc.			0.00	0.00	0.00
Credit Card Payments			0.00	0.00	0.00
TOTALS	$ 150,000.00	$ -	$ 750.00	$ 2,500.00	$ 3,750.00

Pay Yourself First Cash Invested Each Month			Savings Accrued From Free Rental In Duplex $ 750.00	Pay Yourself First PLAN @10% $ 1,250.00	Pay Yourself First PLAN @20% $ 2,500.00
	Plus interest @10%				
ACCRUED Cash 1 Year	10.00		9,900.00	16,500.00	33,000.00
ACCRUED Cash 2 Years	10.00		21,780.00	36,300.00	72,600.00
ACCRUED Cash 3 Years	10.00		34,848.00	58,080.00	116,160.00
ACCRUED Cash 4 Years	10.00		49,222.80	82,038.00	164,076.00
ACCRUED Cash 5 Years	10.00		65,035.08	108,391.80	216,783.60
ACCRUED Cash 6 Years	10.00		82,428.59	137,380.98	274,761.96
ACCRUED Cash 7 Years	10.00		101,561.45	169,269.08	338,538.16
ACCRUED Cash 8 Years	10.00		122,607.59	204,345.99	408,691.97
ACCRUED Cash 9 Years	10.00		145,758.35	242,930.58	485,861.17
ACCRUED Cash 10 Years	10.00		171,224.19	285,373.64	570,747.29
ACCRUED Cash 11 Years	10.00		199,236.60	332,061.01	664,122.01
ACCRUED Cash 12 Years	10.00		230,050.26	383,417.11	766,834.22
ACCRUED Cash 13 Years	10.00		263,945.29	439,908.82	879,817.64
ACCRUED Cash 14 Years	10.00		301,229.82	502,049.70	1,004,099.40
ACCRUED Cash 15 Years	10.00		342,242.80	570,404.67	1,140,809.34
ACCRUED Cash 16 Years	10.00		387,357.08	645,595.14	1,291,190.28
ACCRUED Cash 17 Years	10.00		436,982.79	728,304.65	1,456,609.30
ACCRUED Cash 18 Years	10.00		491,571.07	819,285.12	1,638,570.23
ACCRUED Cash 19 Years	10.00		551,618.18	919,363.63	1,838,727.26
ACCRUED Cash 20 Years	10.00		617,669.99	1,029,449.99	2,058,899.98
ACCRUED Cash 21 Years	10.00		690,326.99	1,150,544.99	2,301,089.98
ACCRUED Cash 22 Years	10.00		770,249.69	1,283,749.49	2,567,498.98
ACCRUED Cash 23 Years	10.00		858,164.66	1,430,274.44	2,860,548.88
ACCRUED Cash 24 Years	10.00		954,871.13	1,591,451.88	3,182,903.76
ACCRUED Cash 25 Years	10.00		1,061,248.24	1,768,747.07	3,537,494.14
ACCRUED Cash 26 Years	10.00		1,178,263.07	1,963,771.78	3,927,543.55
ACCRUED Cash 27 Years	10.00		1,306,979.37	2,178,298.95	4,356,597.91
ACCRUED Cash 28 Years	10.00		1,448,567.31	2,414,278.85	4,828,557.70
ACCRUED Cash 29 Years	10.00		1,604,314.04	2,673,856.73	5,347,713.47
ACCRUED Cash 30 Years	10.00		$ 1,775,635.45	$ 2,959,392.41	$ 5,918,784.82

				10%	20%
			WIFE	$625.00	$1,250.00
			HUSBAND	$625.00	$1,250.00

EXHIBIT 4

PAY YOURSELF FIRST

30 YEAR INVESTMENT EARNINGS ANALYSIS

ITEMS of CONSIDERATION	ANNUAL INCOME	MTHLY. INCOME	MONTHLY SAVINGS 1st DUPLEX PURCHASE	PAY YOURSELF FIRST PLAN @10%	PAY YOURSELF FIRST PLAN @20%
SIGNIFICANT OTHER 1	100,000.00		0.00	0.00	0.00
SIGNIFICANT OTHER 2	80,000.00		0.00	0.00	0.00
Tithes & God's Work @10%			0.00	1,500.00	1,500.00
Pay Yourself First @10 & 20%			0.00	1,500.00	3,000.00
Living Rent Free Mortgage			1,000.00	0.00	0.00
Auto Payment & Expenses			0.00	0.00	0.00
Medical & Life Insurances			0.00	0.00	0.00
Entertainment/Clothing, etc.			0.00	0.00	0.00
Credit Card Payments			0.00	0.00	0.00
TOTALS	$ 180,000.00	$ -	$ 1,000.00	$ 3,000.00	$ 4,500.00

			Savings Accrued From Free Rental in Duplex	Pay Yourself First PLAN @10%	Pay Yourself First PLAN @20%
Pay Yourself First Cash Invested Each Month			$ 1,000.00	$ 1,500.00	$ 3,000.00
	Plus interest @10%				
ACCRUED Cash 1 Year	10.00		13,200.00	19,800.00	39,600.00
ACCRUED Cash 2 Years	10.00		29,040.00	43,560.00	87,120.00
ACCRUED Cash 3 Years	10.00		46,464.00	69,696.00	139,392.00
ACCRUED Cash 4 Years	10.00		65,630.40	98,445.60	196,891.20
ACCRUED Cash 5 Years	10.00		86,713.44	130,070.16	260,140.32
ACCRUED Cash 6 Years	10.00		109,904.78	164,857.18	329,714.35
ACCRUED Cash 7 Years	10.00		135,415.26	203,122.89	406,245.79
ACCRUED Cash 8 Years	10.00		163,476.79	245,215.18	490,430.37
ACCRUED Cash 9 Years	10.00		194,344.47	291,516.70	583,033.40
ACCRUED Cash 10 Years	10.00		228,298.91	342,448.37	684,896.74
ACCRUED Cash 11 Years	10.00		265,648.81	398,473.21	796,946.42
ACCRUED Cash 12 Years	10.00		306,733.69	460,100.53	920,201.06
ACCRUED Cash 13 Years	10.00		351,927.05	527,890.58	1,055,781.16
ACCRUED Cash 14 Years	10.00		401,639.76	602,459.64	1,204,919.28
ACCRUED Cash 15 Years	10.00		456,323.74	684,485.60	1,368,971.21
ACCRUED Cash 16 Years	10.00		516,476.11	774,714.17	1,549,428.33
ACCRUED Cash 17 Years	10.00		582,643.72	873,965.58	1,747,931.16
ACCRUED Cash 18 Years	10.00		655,428.09	983,142.14	1,966,284.28
ACCRUED Cash 19 Years	10.00		735,490.90	1,103,236.35	2,206,472.71
ACCRUED Cash 20 Years	10.00		823,559.99	1,235,339.99	2,470,679.98
ACCRUED Cash 21 Years	10.00		920,435.99	1,380,653.99	2,761,307.98
ACCRUED Cash 22 Years	10.00		1,026,999.59	1,540,499.39	3,080,998.77
ACCRUED Cash 23 Years	10.00		1,144,219.55	1,716,329.33	3,432,658.65
ACCRUED Cash 24 Years	10.00		1,273,161.51	1,909,742.26	3,819,484.52
ACCRUED Cash 25 Years	10.00		1,414,997.66	2,122,496.48	4,244,992.97
ACCRUED Cash 26 Years	10.00		1,571,017.42	2,356,526.13	4,713,052.26
ACCRUED Cash 27 Years	10.00		1,742,639.16	2,613,958.75	5,227,917.49
ACCRUED Cash 28 Years	10.00		1,931,423.08	2,897,134.62	5,794,269.24
ACCRUED Cash 29 Years	10.00		2,139,085.39	3,208,628.08	6,417,256.16
ACCRUED Cash 30 Years	10.00		$ 2,367,513.93	$ 3,551,270.89	$ 7,102,541.78

				10%	20%
			SIGNIFICANT OTHER 1	$833.33	$1,666.67
			SIGNIFICANT OTHER 2	$666.67	$1,333.33

EXHIBIT 5

PAY YOURSELF FIRST - 15-YEAR BUDGET ANALYSIS

NAME:_____ PHONE:_____

ITEMS FOR CONSIDERATION	ANNUAL INCOME	MONTHLY INCOME	CURRENT MONTHLY EXPENSES	NEW BUDGETING PLAN MONTHLY EXPENSES
WIFE				
HUSBAND				
Tithes & God's Work @10%				
PAY YOURSELF FIRST @10%				
Mortgage and/or Rent				
Auto Payment & Insurance				
Gas & Other Auto Expenses				
Life & Medical Insurances				
Utilities, Phone, Cable & Internet				
Food & Household Supplies				
Entertainment & Personal Care				
Educational Loans & Expenses				
Credit Card Payments				
401K & Other Investments				
Other:				
TOTALS	$ -	$ -	$ -	$ -
MONTHLY CASH SURPLUS AFTER ALL EXPENSES HAVE BEEN PAID.			$ -	$ -

			CURRENT MONTHLY SAVINGS	PAY YOURSELF FIRST PLAN @ 10%
On-hand Cash Each Mo.			$ -	$ -
	Plus interest (%)			
ACCRUED Cash 1 Year	2.50		0.00	0.00
ACCRUED Cash 2 Years	3.00		0.00	0.00
ACCRUED Cash 3 Years	3.00		0.00	0.00
ACCRUED Cash 4 Years	3.00		0.00	0.00
ACCRUED Cash 5 Years	3.00		0.00	0.00
ACCRUED Cash 6 Years	3.00		0.00	0.00
ACCRUED Cash 7 Years	3.00		0.00	0.00
ACCRUED Cash 8 Years	3.00		0.00	0.00
ACCRUED Cash 9 Years	3.00		0.00	0.00
ACCRUED Cash 10 Years	3.00		0.00	0.00
ACCRUED Cash 11 Years	3.00		0.00	0.00
ACCRUED Cash 12 Years	3.00		0.00	0.00
ACCRUED Cash 13 Years	3.00		0.00	0.00
ACCRUED Cash 14 Years	3.00		0.00	0.00
ACCRUED Cash 15 Years	3.00		0.00	0.00

EXHIBIT 6 - MANUAL BUDGETING FORM

Order Excel CD or On-line Budgeting Form *@debtterminatorbook.com*

Notice the second most <u>fatal</u> habit & lifestyle of the POOR:

"RENT THEIR DWELLING"

Remember what we learned about the POOR in the first habit & lifestyle; "they spend all of their money as fast as they earn it on things that are mostly rented". Well, here they go! They rent apartments and pay high monthly rentals to a "landlord" who we will be talking about later when we discuss this habit & lifestyle of the RICH. As you may know, apartment rental costs are not tax deductible or reimbursable in any way. This money is down the drain; with no residual value at all, it vanishes without a trace.

Now notice the second fatal habit & lifestyle of the MIDDLE CLASS:

"BUY HOMES BEYOND THEIR FINANCIAL MEANS"

Remember also, what we learned about the *MIDDLE CLASS* in the first habit & lifestyle, "they also spend their money just as fast as they earn it on things that are mostly classified as "LIABILITIES". **Liabilities** are purchases such as clothing, cars, boats, jewelry and even a *PERSONAL HOME* that is not paid off in full. Because the MIDDLE CLASS always opts to buy an expensive personal home; it takes a large portion of their income to cover the monthly mortgage. Usually, after paying the mortgage, they need all of the remaining income to cover their other monthly expenses; which creates a very uneasy situation. How do I cover unexpected emergency costs? Well, this is how families get into debt; then deeper and deeper every time an unexpected cost arises. Why? Because there is no money left over to handle emergencies. And since the MIDDLE CLASS buy more house than they can afford; they usually opt for a 30 year mortgage term just so that they can make the payments manageable. That 30 year home mortgage and the constant borrowing to cover those unanticipated costs, not only, will prevent them from paying themselves first; it will create a serious indebtedness that could be cause for great concern at retirement. Are you beginning to see the reason why these people end up broke after 30 years of earning good money? Under no circumstances should a young couple or a single person for that matter ever buy a personal home on a 30-year mortgage term; a 15-year term makes the best sense at least 90% of the time.

Again, let me repeat, the **POOR** as well as the **MIDDLE CLASS** will end up BROKE after a 30-year work career. Why? It is simply because they make the fatal mistake of not paying themselves first every time they get paid and they spend their money foolishly. The POOR and the MIDDLE CLASS never build up any sub-stantial cash reserves; mainly because of their spending behavior and choices; and therefore, the smallest family emergency or unanticipated expenditure throws them farther and farther behind. These folks will end up broke after working and making good money for 30 years. What a pity.

Now, let's learn and adhere to the second and very important habit & lifestyle practiced by the RICH:

"MAKE THEIR DWELLING A PROFITABLE INVESTMENT"

The Rich pay themselves first a minimum of 10% of their gross income and they **MAKE THEIR DWELLING A PROFITABLE INVESTMENT - NO EXCEPTIONS**! Strict adherence to these first two habits & lifestyles creates a tremendous cash reserve and builds a large net worth model in no time at all. Instead of renting an apartment or buying an expensive personal home with a monthly mortgage and household repairs that drain from its owner of every extra dollar; and then, force its owner to borrow. The RICH opts for investment income property – such as **A DUPLEX!** What's a DULPEX you might ask? It's a two-family dwelling whereby the owner buys the duplex, moves into one side of the dwelling and rents out the other side to a POOR person. You remember the POOR people that we discussed above who rented their dwelling. You also remember the landlord that rented the dwelling to the POOR person. Here, the RICH is the owner, also called the "Landlord". The renter or POOR person pays rent which covers the monthly mortgage for the owner or RICH person. Therefore, the RICH person lives in the duplex free; **thus, the dwelling is a profitable investmen**t. The money saved from not having to pay for dwelling can be saved or invested in another DUPLEX or in some other wise money making venture. "Money making Money", are you starting to see why the RICH keeps getting richer and why the POOR keeps getting poorer? It's mainly, because the POOR keep giving their money to the RICH as fast as they earn it. It's so simple, isn't it? It matters not how much money you make, what matters is how much you keep.

IT'S NOT ROCKET SCIENCE, IT'S JUST COMMON SENSE.

Notice the third habit & lifestyle of the POOR:

"WORK FOR MONEY - EMPLOYEES WORKING AN 8 TO 5 JOBS"

Again, let's review what we've learned about the POOR in the first two habits & lifestyles; "they spend their money as fast as they earn it on things that are mostly rented". They rent apartments and pay high rental to a "landlord" (The RICH). We also discovered that apartment rental costs are not tax deductible; nor are they reimbursable in any way. The money spent for rent is totally down the drain with no residual value at all. Any money paid for rent, in essence, just vanishes without a trace. What is the source of the poor folks money? The POOR are employees who work 8 hours per day and usually 5 days per week for a total of 40 hours. Normally, they have no other income sources; except for occasional over-time-pay. They are pretty much trapped in a fixed income with very little desire or motivation to change their situation. They settle for and embrace the *get-by-from-paycheck-to-paycheck* mentality. And there you have it.

IT IS, WHAT IT IS.

Now notice the third habit & lifestyle of the MIDDLE CLASS:

"WORK FOR MONEY - EMPLOYEES WORKING AN 8 TO 5 JOBS"

What have we learned about the MIDDLE CLASS in the first two habits & lifestyles? Well, they also spend their money just as fast as they earn it; but on stuff that makes them look rich, *"LIABILITIES".* We learned that *"LIABILITIES"* are purchases such as clothing, cars, boats, jewelry and even **PERSONAL HOMES** that are not paid off in full. Unlike the POOR, the MIDDLE CLASS buy expensive personal homes with large monthly mortgage payments which accounts for the lion's share of their income. We also know that home repair costs and other family emergencies cause a major indebtedness scenario for the MIDDLE CLASS. Why? Because they allow the purchase of the home to over extend their income capacity and no money is left over to handle unplanned expenditures. Paying themselves first is out of the question and they can kiss any hopes of building up a savings or any cash reserve good-bye. What caused this disastrous existence? The 30-year mortgage payment on the personal home that is usually way beyond their financial means creates a hole so deep that they can never get out of working an 8 to 5 job.

The least stressful and obvious alternative is to just settle for the **"getting-by-from-paycheck-to-paycheck"** mentality. In other words, I'll just try and keep my head above the water line; or I'll keep praying for a miracle; or maybe I'll hit the lottery; or someone may die and leave me a significant inheritance in their WILL. And there you are – sadly, it is what it is.

My wife, Miss Donna, and I teach a **DEBT FREE LIVING SUNDAY SCHOOL CLASS** at our church. The pastor at our church, perceiving the negative impact of a world's sagging economy on his church membership and the community that surrounded it, felt that it might be a beneficial and worth-while idea to begin a **MINISTRY** that helps people to deal with their financial needs and frustrations. The church does a great job in addressing spiritual needs; however, many Christians, we believe, could become even better stewards for the kingdom given more adequate financial resources. And ideally, this ministry could also have a positive impact on the church's financial growth and its ability to reach a much larger group or audience; everybody wins, truly a win/win scenario. Our Pastor discussed the Debt Free Living **MINISTRY** idea with us and we agreed to develop the course of study based on our own **RAGS TO RICHES** experiences. Both my wife and I came from very deprived beginnings and have been able to achieve financial independence in a very short timeframe just by practicing and strictly adhering to the habits & lifestyles of the RICH as we are outlining for your use.

I share that little history with you only to allow you insight into the story that I'm about to tell: There was a couple in one of our Debt Free Living Sunday School Classes that epitomizes the plight and dilemmas that befall most **MIDDLE CLASS** dwellers. This story will depress some, inspire others and cause many of you to feel glad, thankful and fortunate that this is not the situation in your life. If you are living the habits & lifestyles of the RICH, you will be amazed that people can be so unwise in their financial planning. If you are living the habits & lifestyles of the MIDDLE CLASS, you will finally understand what went terribly wrong in your life. And, if you are living the habits & lifestyles of the POOR, you should hopefully be inspired to make the giant leap from your current habits & lifestyles to those habits & lifestyles practiced by the RICH. To protect their privacy and to maintain the confidentiality privilege that we assure all of our students, we'll call this couple **Mr. & Mrs. "X".**

MR. & MRS. "X" - A TRUE STORY

They are either in their late 40's or early 50's; age is very hard to predict with some people.   They do not pool their money; and each of them has his or her group of monthly bills to pay.   In strictest confidence, Mr. "X" came to us and he shared his portion of the couple's monthly expenditures.   He wished to see if we could assist him with his stressful and most difficult financial dilemma.   His annual income was in excess of $ 82,000 per year; but because of a 401k loan and various other payroll deductions, he only brought home a net monthly amount of **$3,072.**   Mr. "X" provided us a list detailing the monthly obligations for which he was responsible.   No surprise, heading the list of monthly expenditures was their Home Mortgage Payment - $1,680; car payments - $408; car insurance & expenses - $350;   home equity loan - $155; utilities & phone $405; maid & security service - $165; and credit cards - $800; for a total monthly expenditure of **$3963**.

It is painfully obvious that Mr. "X" can not meet his monthly obligation. In fact, he is **$891** short or in the hole, so to speak.   How could he possibly have gotten himself into this awful fix? What was he thinking? Is this a true story or is the author just exaggerating the truth for effect? I assure you that this is a true story up to and including the **MAID**. A maid? Yes, a **MAID**. As you think about Mr. X's dilemma, think about the cause and effect in this situation. His house payment or mortgage is over one-half of his net income which is not good financial planning. His other must or necessary expenses used up all of his remaining monthly net-pay income; which leaves him unable to handle any unexpected costs. Therefore, when an emergency, such as, a furnace break-down; in order to fix that broken furnace Mr. "X" had to **"CHARGE IT"**; and the problem grew worse and worse as each emergency arose. Before long, he had dug a **DEBT PIT** so deep that only God himself could help him. In other words, he needed a miracle. Why didn't Mr. "X" just get a second job? Well, he said he couldn't because he volunteers at the church, and he was currently going to school to learn how to become a better volunteer. You laugh, but I'm being very serious. To the MIDDLE CLASS it is very important to them that they look successful; never mind, that their world is falling down around them as we speak.

You see, as long as their MIDDLE CLASS friends, who are probably living the same disastrous existence, think well of them they are okay. What a deplorable life; when you really think about the life of many MIDDLE CLASS people, it may be better to be poor. At least the POOR don't have all of that baggage to carry. They don't have to live a fake life of lies. And I believe the POOR can make the transition to the habits & lifestyles of the RICH more readily and easily. Here's a fact that might surprise you; our class was made up of mostly POOR people; even though the MIDDLE CLASS needed the DEBT FREE concepts that were being taught more so than the POOR. This is just our opinion, the **MIDDLE CLASS** felt that some of their MIDDLE CLASS friends might see them attending a Debt Free Living class and they might think that they were in debt. Therefore, rather than chance embarrass-ment they opted not to participate. I'm in bad shape, but I can't let anybody know. I need help, but if I ask for help they may find out the truth about me. I'll just ride it out. It could be worse.

Again, let me reiterate, the **POOR** as well as the **MIDDLE CLASS** will end up BROKE after a 30-year work career. Why? It is simply because they make the fatal mistake of not paying themselves first every time they get paid. The POOR and the MIDDLE CLASS never build up any substantial cash reserves mainly because of their spending behavior and choices; and therefore, the smallest family emergency or unanticipated expenditures throw them farther and farther behind. They work 8 to 5 jobs on a fixed income and they have no other source of income.

It is what it is; however, there's **GOOD NEWS**, you can choose to live the habits & lifestyles of the RICH.

Now, let's learn and adhere to the third habit & lifestyle practiced by the RICH:

"MAKE THEIR MONEY WORK FOR THEM & HAVE OTHERS WOKING FOR THEM"

The Rich pay themselves first a minimum of 10% of their gross income and **MAKE THEIR DWELLING A PROFITABLE INVESTMENT - NO EXCEPTIONS!!!** We've demonstrated how strict adherence to these first two habits & lifestyles alone can create tremendous cash reserves, riches and financial independence, if you will. A young person who buys a personal home as his/her first priority is making a decision that will delay achievement of financial independence in their life. In the long term it would be a far better plan, financially speaking, to buy a DUPLEX and live in it rent free. As we've already learned, renting an apartment or buying an expensive personal home with a monthly mortgage and household repairs that drain from its owner every extra dollar which forces the borrowing habit, does not seem to be very appealing. The RICH opts for investments in income property (DUPLEX) as their first priority; a move that guarantees great financial returns. The RICH will live in the duplex for *FREE;* and the money gains as a result of not having to pay rent or mortgage can be saved or invested towards the acquisition of a second DUPLEX or in some other wise money making ventures.   In this third habit & lifestyle of RICH, **MONEY MAKING MONEY IS THE NAME OF THE GAME.**   Your money can't work for you until, a significant cash base or cash reserve can be established.   Since we all know that money attracts money, the RICH utilizes the first two habits & lifestyles as a money generating engine.   These two habits & lifestyles produce a money generating engine that will run and produce money for its owner for as long as its owner practices these two habits & lifestyles.   This is too simple you say. Sure it's simple, but most people miss this simple money making process because they don't practice the **"first two very key"** habits & lifestyles of the RICH:

<u>**PAY YOURSELF FIRST**</u>
&
<u>**MAKE YOUR DWELLING A PROFITABLE INVESTMENT**</u>

These two practices provide the **"SEEDS"** from which all other significant blessings from God can grow.   These first two practices (habits & lifestyles) provide the resources needed to make this third habit & lifestyle come alive.

MAKE THEIR MONEY WORK FOR THEM & HAVE OTHERS WOKING FOR THEM

Making money earn more money is the secret to it all. Once significant cash reserves have been established, there are virtually unlimited business opportunities available to those who have liquid cash resources. Starting a successful business and having others working for you is, without a doubt, one of the best and quickest ways to amass a fortune in wealth. The RICH are constantly looking for business ventures or opportunities. You will find the RICH working 8 to 5 jobs just as a stepping stone to starting their own business. Many wise investments avail themselves to those who have significant and ready cash reserves. The idea of buying income or rental property has always been and continues to be a very lucrative investment for individuals and small business investors.

There are so many ways to make your money work for you provided you have a significant amount to work with. And there are so many others willing to work for you, and make money for you, if you have the vision to create your own business.

As almost everyone knows **Bill Gates**, **Donald Trump** and **Oprah Winfrey**, three of the riches people alive today, all started out with a vision and an unwavering desire to be successful. To become a successful entrepreneur in this country, a college degree is highly recommended and, of course, can certainly be of great value; but **NOT REQUIRED**, as Bill Gates and this author have proven beyond the shadow of any doubt. Desire and passion can help anyone overcome any preconceived shortcomings such as a lack of education, environmental restraints, physical limitations, mental imprisonments, racial barriers, and all the other convenient and maybe, politically correct, "excuses" that people sometimes use to justify failure. If you truly want it bad enough; and if you have an unwavering desire to get it; whatever "it" may be, the mind will formulate or develop a **plan** or a **strategy** to make it so. Speaking of DESIRE, let's continue our discussion of the next critical habit & lifestyle which has to do with desire or lack there of.

The fourth habit & lifestyle of the POOR:

"NO DESIRE TO BE RICH (RELATES GODLINESS WITH POVERTY)"

Again, let's review what we've learned about the POOR. They don't pay themselves first, they rent almost everything they have, and they spend their hard earned money as fast as they earn it. And now we discover the true and bona fide reason why the poor are POOR; they HAVE NO DESIRE TO BE RICH. End of story? No not yet, there are a few other key habits & lifestyles practiced by the POOR that we need to examine in order to help others understand what to watch out for. A lack of desire has killed so many lives and destroyed so many dreams. "No desire" is a most deadly disease of the spirit that creates emptiness and nothingness that can affect us all in ways unimaginable. I'm sure that each of us has, at one time or another, experienced persons who just had no desire to do, or to be anything. These persons can be so depressing that if you are not careful their depressions can rub-off on you. I believe a lack of desire is almost sinful and it can rob people of their freedom, their self-esteem and their potential. I'm sorry, but it is what it is. It is almost impossible to achieve wealth without desire. Desire is the key that opens the door to everything. You got to want it before you can achieve it.

Okay! the fourth habit & lifestyle of the MIDDLE CLASS:

"HAVE A WHIMPY DESIRE TO BE RICH; NO REAL COMMITMENT"

Let's get ourselves up to date relative to the **MIDDLE CLASS.** Remember, they *Pay Themselves Last*, if any money is left over after expenses; they *buy personal homes beyond their financial means* and they spend their money just as fast as they earn it. And now we see that they only **HAVE A WHIMPY DESIRE TO BE RICH.** We've also learned that the desire to look rich is the more substantial to the MIDDLE CLASS than the desire to actually be rich. For this reason alone, the **MIDDLE CLASS** buy things that help them achieve this end, i.e. extravagant and expensive cars, personal homes, jewelry furs and etc. All these items are purchased mainly for the sole purpose of deceiving the public. In other words, to make their owner look rich and successful. Isn't that silly? The MIDDLE CLASS buy all these liabilities on credit and if they lose their 8 to 5 jobs, all these thing could be taken away. This group lives from day to day, month to month and year to year on the edge. They live on a hope and a prayer that nothing adverse happens in their near future. Such as: I pray that I don't lose my job. I pray that nothing breaks down. I pray and hope that, someday, I can get a better job; otherwise, my children will not be able to go to college. And oh, I almost forgot my daughter's wedding; oh my God, what am I going to do?

Don't be deceived! Now, the rich have all the things that the poor and the middle class struggle so hard to have and much more. However, the rich always put first-things-first, they *achieved wealth first*; then, they buy all the "desires of their hearts" when they are able to pay cash for their purchases. No interest, no monthly bills, no stress, just enjoy the ride that a life of wealth offers. It all starts with Desire!!

Now, let's learn and adhere to the fourth and very crucial habit & lifestyle practiced by the RICH:

"HAVE AN UNWAVERING DESIRE TO BE RICH"

The rich *PAY THEMSELVES FIRST* a minimum of 10% of their gross income; they *MAKE THEIR DWELLING A PROFITABLE INVESTMENT;* they *MAKE THEIR MONEY WORK FOR THEM* and *HAVE OTHERS WORKING FOR THEM;* and now, they *HAVE AN UNWAVERING DESIRE TO BE RICH!!!!!!*
NO EXCEPTIONS!

TO ACHIEVE IT, YOU'VE GOT TO WANT IT BAD ENOUGH TO SURRENDER YOUR LIFE TO IT.   WHATEVER IT MAY BE.   IN THIS CASE, IT IS THE PURSUIT OF WEALTH.

Are you starting to understand how the RICH get to be rich and how they maintain and grow their wealth?   Everything they do creates wealth in one way or another. Their unwavering desire to achieve great wealth causes their minds to develop creative plans and strategies that perceive the making of money as its first and foremost priority.

The unwavering desire of the RICH compels them to adhere to the first four Habits & Lifestyles because that is where the money is made.   The poor and the middle class ignore these first four Habits & Lifestyles; by so doing, they condemn or sentence themselves to a *life existence without wealth and riches*.   The RICH want it, they need it, they must have it, and they can't live without it; to be without it is to be poor. ***To be poor is not a viable option for the rich.***

For the RICH, the first three habits & lifestyles are the ***money generating engines*** that will produce money for its owner for as long as the owner practices these habits & lifestyles.   The fourth Habit & Lifestyle - ***AN UNWAVERING DESIRE TO BE RICH*** -provides the fuel that makes these ***money generating engines*** work flawlessly.

My friends as you read this book take these lessons very serious.   For, if you would but adhere to and follow the clear and simple Habits & Lifestyles of the RICH you will achieve what the RICH have achieved; wealth and prosperity, freedom and influence, happiness and great joy, ability to make a difference in the world, endless and awesome opportunities to help and bless others.   And possibly most importantly of all, you will please your creator immensely and he will show you favor and continue to bless you with even more and more of the same (Matt. 25:14-29).

LET'S SEE WHERE WE ARE AT THIS POINT IN OUR JOURNEY.

The first four Habits & Lifestyles dealt with:

➢ **THE CREATION AND THE ACQUISITION OF MONEY.**

The last three Habits & Lifestyles will deal with:

➢ **THE PROTECTION AND THE MAINTENANCE OF MONEY.**

As we have discovered, the first four Habits & Lifestyles practiced by the RICH make the acquisition of money possible and easy. Once the money has been successfully acquired, the last three Habits & Lifestyles saves, maintains, protects and guards the money from loss. Expenditures must be controlled else the money will leave out as fast as it came in; which is a big mistake made by the **POOR** and **MIDDLE CLASS**. They spend more than they make which means not only do they not have any money, they are in a money deficit or shortage, to put it kindly. But for the sake of our young reader, let's call it what it is – **DEBT**. Debt is bad!!! Debt is an addictive disease which can destroy dreams and families. Bankruptcy is not a good thing either; however for some it can help create a new start when all else has failed. If for some reason, you find yourself in an indebtedness situation that has totally consumed all of your financial resources; and you can see no clear way out no matter what you try, I strongly recommend seeking a new start. Most folks who find themselves buried in a sea of debt did not create that dreadful situation alone, they had help. Credit card companies are sometimes just as much to blame as the credit card users themselves. Credit card companies in an effort to attract young and inexperience consumers will develop all kinds of marketing incentive plans and schemes, which most likely will change in their favor once the consumer is hooked. The RICH people are wise to these credit card scams and incentive marketing approaches, and they avoid them by PAYING CASH for everything they buy. It's the interest rates on credit and credit cards debt that get people into trouble.

Let's cut to the chase, if you somehow find yourself in too deep and you can see no way out, you should file bankruptcy and create for yourself a fresh new start. Now, the next time around, hopefully, you will have learned your lesson and you will adhere to all of the Habits & Lifestyles of the rich – NO EXCEPTIONS. Once you are out of debt, PLEASE, be smart and do not fall for those schemes and tricks that the credit card companies are planning just for you and people like you. Don't be fooled again into believing that you can handle or manage the debt. Be wise and learn some patience; wait until you can pay cash and then negotiate a good price for your money. Change your Habits & Lifestyles to that of the RICH --- Choose to be RICH!!! Being rich is great; it is one of the most wonderful feelings that life offers. Rags to Riches is an incredible journey that is worth all of the pain, all of the suffering and all of the personal sacrifices that is required in order to successfully complete this marvelous and most rewarding endeavor. The journey is worth the effort; we know, for we have successfully completed the trip. With the knowledge you are being given here, you or anyone, for that matter, can successfully make this Rags to Riches journey. Decide today, that you seriously want it. Follow the Habits & Lifestyles practiced by the rich and go get it for yourself and for your family. That truly is the smart thing to do and you'll be so glad and proud that you did.

The fifth Habit & Lifestyle of the POOR:

"CREDIT CARDS – ALL OVER THE LIMIT WITH VERY HIGH INTEREST RATE"

When a credit card is used, you the purchaser loses. Why? When buying on credit, you lose any ability to negotiate the final purchase price; thereby, giving up any possibility to stretch your money. We will discuss this <u>money stretching feature</u> later on under the Habit & Lifestyle of the RICH, where it will have more meaning. The POOR have no purchasing clout; nor do they have any possibility of making their buying situation anything other than what is on the price tag. You see, the price tags on merchandise are really there for the POOR. "Take it or leave it", you have nothing that would motivate me, the merchant, to negotiate with you. Plus, because the merchandise is being charged, the poor must pay an additional 12% to 23.5 % in interest charges. In other words, buying a $100 item on credit could cost the POOR up to $123.50. Isn't that just a terrible scenario for the POOR people amongst us? On the surface, it does not seem very fair. Yes, I really feel badly about it, but *IT IS WHAT IT IS.* For the poor there is an answer, but they've got to want it – *embrace the habits & lifestyles of the Rich*.

The fifth Habit & Lifestyle of the MIDDLE CLASS:

"CREDIT CARDS –
PAYING MINIMUM MONTHLY CHARGES, NO END IN SIGHT"

The plight of the MIDDLE CLASS is not much different. They have a slight advantage as compared to the poor; in that, they usually have better credit ratings which allow them to negotiate better interest rates on their credit cards. Still, they get to pay that same price that's on the price tag. They too, have very little clout with merchants.   To the merchant, it's still a purchase on credit; which means he has to wait for his money from the credit card company; he in most cases has to pay the credit card company a fee for each transaction. To the merchant, as it is to all business-minded people; time is money, and if you can get the money to me faster it is worth something to me.   That's what makes negotiating come alive!!!   Are you starting to see how the advantages seem to always favor the RICH and how the old saying about, "money talks and B.S. walks" applies. If one has money, money comes to him with great ease; if one has no money, money will flee from him in a great hurry. For more insight regarding the flight of money, read these scriptures: Matt. 13:12, Matt. 25:29, Mark 4:25, Luke 8:18 & Luke 19:26

Now, let's learn and adhere to the fifth Habit & Lifestyle practiced by the RICH:

"PAY CASH - NEGOTIATE PRICING –
ONE CREDIT CARD FOR EMERGENCY USE"

In an effort to add more emphasis and magnitude to my point, permit me to repeat myself, everything that RICH people do is motivated by money and the attraction of the same. Paying cash creates financial benefits and opportunities for the rich:

- ALLOWS ENORMOUS LATITUDE IN NEGOTIATIONS
- AVOIDS ALL COSTS ASSOCIATED WITH CREDIT, i.e. INTERESTS & etc.
- STRETCHES THEIR MONEY
- CONTROLS THEIR EXPENDITURES
- INCREASES THEIR PURCHASING POWER
- MAKES AND SAVES THEIR MONEY.

Unlike the POOR and MIDDLE CLASS, the RICH has mammoth clout with merchants; and therefore, the merchants are able and willing to negotiate pricing. You see now things have changed from what they were when the merchant dealt with the Poor and the Middle Class. Why? Remember the old saying about money talks, well here's the proof. Just imagine a RICH consumer out shopping for products and services that he is in need of. Since he is paying cash, and he desires no credit consideration, his negotiation strategy with the local merchant would probably go something like this: "Mr. Merchant, I see that this item has a price tag of $100; however, since I have cash money, how much can you discount this item for me today? (or) Mr. Merchant, I have exactly $75 and I am interested in buying this $100 item, will you sell it to me for that price or must I buy it some place else? (or) I will buy two of your $100 items and pay cash if you approve a 50% discount". Having cash has allowed him in one case to buy $100 worth of product for $75, and in another case to buy $200 worth of product for $100 or half price. This is a good example of an advantage that avails itself only because of the possession of cash; an option that is rarely available to the poor and middle class. Negotiating is a tool used by a buyer to get the asking price reduced. If one is a successful negotiator, he/she can save a lot of money or put another way, "stretch his/her money".

Example: A Jeep SUV (Sport Utility Vehicle) - asking price = $25,000.

The POOR, buying on credit, will more likely than not pay close to the asking price.

Likewise, the MIDDLE CLASS, buying on credit, would also pay close to asking price.

The RICH would be in a good position to negotiate the price and pay for less; since they can *pay cash*.

I can almost hear the Rich consumer starting his negotiation bid right about now. If you listen closely, you may be able to hear the rich buyer's voice to as he starts to size-up the car dealer. The Rich buyer, who is very well dressed in a dark suit, white shirt and a bright red tie, he begins to speak:

"Mr. Car Dealer, how much will you discount the asking price of this Jeep SUV, since I have cash and can buy this SUV today"?

(or)

"Mr. Car Dealer will you discount the asking price of this SUV by 20% or must I take my cash and buy from your competitor across the street"?

Just so that you know Mr. Car Dealer, I'm going to buy an SUV from someone with my cash today. It does not have to be from you; it can be from any dealer who is willing to meet my terms. Listen, if I'm wasting your time or irritating you with my persistence, just let me know and I'm on my way.

Look at them!! Can't you just see that car salesperson and his sales manager scrambling to put a deal together for the rich buyer? Having sold no cars yet today, there is no way they will let that cash walk away. Cash money is powerful and people listen to cash. Paying Cash absolutely saves and makes you money, if you have the skills and the patience to negotiate.

NEGOTIATING, simply put, is the art of competing for blessings! God places blessings before us and allows us to compete for them. He does not care who wins; since all of us are his children. He wants to bless us all abundantly; however, we control our blessing flow. If we are good negotiators, our flow is great; if not; then the flow is less.

Now on to the one credit card suggestion, having one credit card is a must, JUST IN CASE your money is stolen or it runs out and you are not at home. You want to avoid risking your safety as well as the safety of your family when possible. Therefore, the one credit card for emergencies is a good practice. For example, those car rental companies who require a credit card and refuse to take cash payments. Isn't that silly? The one credit card also comes in handy for other purchase where you are not sure about the quality, warranty and return policies of products. We recommend a credit card that requires payment in full at the end of each month; which helps keep spending at a level that can be easily controlled. The American Express Gold Card meets all of our requirements and more. If for some reason, the American Express Card is not possible for you, shop around for a credit card company that offers you the lowest interest rates.

The key here is to pay cash for all purchases and make sure that the things being acquired are truly needed and will add value to your life. The RICH are always looking to buy product or goods that produce income and profit. In other word, items or things that appreciate in value as time pass on. The items being described here are called **ASSETS.** We will discuss **ASSETS** and **LIABILITIES** in the next group of Habits & Lifestyles. Once again, we will be examining the buying behaviors and practices of our three groups – The Poor, The Middle Class and The Rich.

The sixth Habit & Lifestyle of the POOR:

"BUY NEITHER ASSETS NOR LIABILITIES (RENT MOST THINGS)"

The POOR usually leave no permanent foot-prints in the sand. It's as though they were never here. They rent almost everything they use during their stay here on earth; and when they die, it all goes back to the owner. It's much like leasing a car. You drive it and make lease payment on it for 3 or 4 years and then it goes back to the owner and you have nothing to show for all that money spent on lease payments. Isn't that kind of silly, when you truly think about it? The owner, who is usually from the RICH group, is the only one that achieves a profit or financial advantage in these rental and leasing transactions. At the end of these transactions, the POOR gets absolutely nothing. This is a very sad commentary indeed. Why would anyone do something so **UNINTELLIGENT** (to be kind) so **STUPID** (to be less kind)? This particular Habit & Lifestyle played a major role in our motivation to write this book. We see so many people, whom we care for very deeply going down this path. It is our sincere hope that this book; which has been written in very simple terms, will help people to see how easy it can be to change from their current destructive **HABITS & LIFESTYLES** and opt for the wise and proven **HABITS & LIFESTYLES** of the RICH.

The sixth Habit & Lifestyle of the MIDDLE CLASS:

<u>"BUY LIABILITIES: PERSONAL HOMES, BOATS, CARS, CLOTHES, JEWELRY & ETC."</u>

The plight of the MIDDLE CLASS is much different in this Habit & Lifestyle. They take the opposing position as compared to the poor; in that, they don't rent or lease. They purchase everything, which is good in itself; however, what they end up purchasing are usually products categorized as liabilities. While buying liabilities is still a far better option than renting, they can get their owner in deep trouble if some negative adversity comes upon the owner without warning. For instance let's say, the owner loses his income source or his job; he could then lose all of his liabilities that are not paid off. Once some **Liabilities** are paid-off-in-full, such as personal homes, they switch to the **assets** column. The MIDDLE CLASS always seem to over extend in the area of home buying. With the middle class, there is usually no sound budget planning in place; buying on credit, with the continual and tempting availability of credit cards; and before long the spending situation quickly gets out of hand. With everything going out and very little coming in; financial disaster is just around the corner.

Now, with almost any unexpected emergency, this train is off the track, so to speak. And this feeble Middle Class "sap" is worst off than his POOR partner who rents everything.   I can tell that you are starting to get the picture and you are starting to see clearly my point.   I can see that you don't want any parts of those Habits & Lifestyles practiced by the POOR and the MIDDLE CLASS.   You are going to change your Habits & Lifestyles to those practiced by the RICH because you are smart and you want better for yourself and your family.   That is a very wise decision and you'll be very happy that you made it.   Money comes with great ease to the man who has much and flees quickly from those who have little.   Again, for more insight on this very clear and precise biblical decree which deals with those who have and those who have not, read the following Biblical Scriptures:

Matt. 13:12, Matt. 25:29, Mark 4:25, Luke 8:18 & Luke 19:26

At this point, I want you to take a break from this book; get your Bible, hopefully the King James Version, and read all of these scriptures; then return back to this book and begin here where you left off.   Having you go directly to the Bible saves me from having to copy all of those very powerful and telling scriptures into this text.   I think it's always more inspirational and more meaningful to get it first-hand from the **HOLY BIBLE**.   Now that you are back from your Biblical assignment; let's begin again:

Again, let's learn and adhere to the sixth Habit & Lifestyle of the RICH:

"BUY ASSETS: INCOME PROPERTY, LAND, STOCKS, MUTUAL FUNDS & ETC."

Again, for the sake of adding even more emphasis and more proof relative to my observation, permit me to repeat myself one last time; everything that RICH people do is motivated by money and the attraction of the same.   They buy assets for the obvious financial advantages that assets represent. Assets are added sources of income that assist its owner's efforts to amass wealth. ASSETS are almost like having a second person work along side you and give you all of the money that he makes.   It's like having a safety net so that in case you lose your job or your main source of income, your ASSETS will continue to work hard every day and give you all of their earnings with no questions asked and no complaining.   The Biblical book of Matthew starting in Chapter 25 and Verses 14 - 29 should be read in its entirety. My intent and purpose here is to help you understand that when you practice the Habits & Lifestyles of the RICH, **GOD THE MASTER AND RULER OVER ALL THINGS**, will help you by showing you favor as the Master did with the first two servants in the Parable of Talents.   On the other hand, when you practice the Habits & Lifestyles of the POOR and the MIDDLE CLASS, **GOD THE MASTER AND RULER OVER**

<u>ALL THINGS</u>, will be disappointed in you and **not** show you favor as the Master did not with the third servant in the Parable of Talents.

The freedom of choice is given to everyone at birth. Freely a life is given and what we choose to do with that life either pleases our Master or it disappoints Him. Still, the choice is ours to make; whether Poor and worthless, Middle Class and ineffective or Rich and wise; enjoy-ing all of the favor and the celebration of a God that is exceedingly pleased with your accomplishments. We must all make choices; some will be difficult and some not so difficult.

Sadly, most people take the seemingly easy road that's traveled by the POOR and the MIDDLE CLASS simply because those roads require very little commitment; almost no planning is necessary, and it's just a "willey" "nilley" existence; "catch as catch can" walk through a life that makes very little difference and blesses no one. Then finally death comes and the family is left struggling financially trying to bury the loser; while all the time, feeling for him for living life so irresponsibly and stupid.

ONCE AGAIN, IT IS WHAT IT IS!

The seventh Habit & Lifestyle of the POOR:

"DON'T SEEK ADVICE – JUMP IN BLINDLY WITHOUT KNOWLEDGE"

The POOR just don't seem to get it. They defy all the laws of good common sense and deductive reasoning. I am simply amazed at how people who live in America, the land of opportunity, can fall into this senseless existence and position of being POOR. However, if you review their Habits & Lifestyles you can readily see that their troubles come as a result of some very bad choices, i.e. they don't pay themselves first. More simply put, they spend "all" of their money as fast as they make it on stuff that will return no value to them. They live their lives almost like the animals, devouring everything as though there is no tomorrow. Although, some animals like the squirrels put away food for the winter; which truly is an act of paying themselves first. Even Squirrels are wise enough not to eat all of their nuts as fast as they find them; they put some aside for hard times. The POOR are seemingly so full of pride that they seek no advice or help from those who are knowledgeable about financial matters. Therefore, they are never made aware of proven techniques and rules for acquiring wealth and riches. Maybe it's simply a pride issue. I'm not sure.

It would be totally inconsiderate and irresponsible of me to make the mistake of lumping all poor people and all middle class people together without recognizing that there are extenuating circumstances and life misfortunes whereby a person or persons have very little control over their fate; such as a prolonged illness, lost of employment for a long period of time, a divorce where literally everything was justly or unjustly taken away, an unexpected or sudden death of the family's bread-winner and etc. These situations are understandable and I offer my sincere apologies if this book has offended persons of this faction who find themselves in a poverty stricken predicament created through no fault of their own. I trust that this book has helped you to at least see that there is light at the end of the tunnel. If you adhere to the principles shared in this book and if you have faith and believe that with God all things are possible, there is a way out even for you....

The seventh Habit & Lifestyle of the MIDDLE CLASS:

"TAKE ADVICE FROM FRIENDS, FAMILY & CHURCH FOLKS"

The MIDDLE CLASS usually seek bad advice because the advice is no better than its source.   For instance, if you needed brain surgery, would you go to a carpenter or a truck driver for advice? **NO!** You would go to a brain surgeon. It amazes me to see people talking to people about money matters who are in worst shape financially than they are. What's even more astounding is the notion that these same people use that advice to make life choices.   The MIDDLE CLASS do this all the time.   Ask them why and their response usually is "that is what my mom did" or "so and so from church said" or" my brother Steve told me".   Don't ask me why or what would posses anyone to take advice from people who have no clue. I don't know why, they just do.   Maybe this explains why the middle class have so many financial miscues and set-backs.   When you put this action in the proper prospective, seeking financial advice from uninformed people is on the same scale as that of letting a truck driver perform brain surgery, the patient would surely die.   Isn't that silly? I hope this book will save someone from financial suicide.

Finally, let's learn and adhere to the seventh Habit & Lifestyle practiced by the RICH:

"SEEK ADVICE FROM COMPETENT & WEALTHY PEOPLE"

The RICH seek advice from those who are RICH; those who have proven track records and certified documentation to substantiate their competence. This is not rocket science, it's just good common sense. Why would you take financial advice from someone who is in the process of filing bankruptcy? You wouldn't unless you were totally unwise or just plain stupid.

This section is primarily targeted and aimed at young high school and college graduates who are getting prepared to start their lives in the real world; and for the first time, starting to make their own choices. Every parent would be wise to get a copy of this very no-nonsense, straight-forward book in the hands of their children before they leave home for the first time. Unfortunately, schools and colleges do not teach life concepts that will help their students understand the financial ramifications of their choices. The lifestyle choices made, whether informed or not, will lead to a definite path of either riches or poverty.

Without knowledge such as that imparted in this book, our youths will continue to stumble into and through life blindly with no road map to guide their way. The reason why so many people end up poor is because of the knowledge base with which they are most familiar? No one is teaching our students the concepts and the benefits of paying themselves first, paying cash, negotiating for best price, making their dwelling a profitable investment, starting their own business and saving their money. Students are being taught how to be good consumers – spenders and borrowers. Once out on their own, these newly trained consumers are set-up for the kill. TV commercials are without a doubt the biggest contributor to the spending and debt epidemic. These commercials encourage irresponsible spending by providing endless product offerings along with world class advertising campaigns that present great motivation to the unskilled and uninformed perspective buyer. The great chase of the, so called, **AMERICAN DREAM** is the next biggest contributor to this epidemic. You must review very carefully **THE AMERICAN DREAM** vs **THE DREAM OF THE WISE** that is found on the next pages. If you let **THE DREAM OF THE WISE** become the foundation of your thinking, you will be able to avoid many of the societal and consumer traps that most will encounter.

Strict adherence to the **(7) HABITS & LIFESTYLES** practiced by the RICH will safeguard you from all the pitfalls and schemes developed for the sole purpose of convincing you to spend all of your hard-earned money.   Unfortunately, the POOR and the MIDDLE CLASS will fall for these schemes and they will spend "all" of their hard-earned money as fast as they earn it. They will work all their lives and will end up broke and wonder what went wrong; unless they wake up and get themselves better equipped financially. The choice is yours to make.   We have given you all the tools that you will need; however if it is to be it is up to you.   Always remember that, it matters not how much **MONEY** you make; it's how much **MONEY** you keep, of that which you make.

NOT ROCKET SCIENCE, JUST COMMON SENSE!

RESULTS OF
THE AMERICAN DREAM

POOR & MIDDLE CLASS   **UNHAPPY & BROKE**

VS

RESULTS OF
THE DREAM OF THE WISE

RICH & HAPPY!!!   **LOTS OF MONEY!!!**

THE AMERICAN DREAM

GO TO COLLEGE & GET A GOOD EDUCATION

GRADUATE & GET A GOOD JOB THAT PAYS WELL

GET MARRIED & BUY THE HOUSE OF YOUR DREAMS

OPT FOR A 30-YR MORTGAGE TO KEEP PAYMENTS LOW

WORK FOR 30 YEARS, GET A WATCH AND THEN RETIRE POOR

MEDICARE, MEDICAID, SOCIAL SECURITY AND PENSION PLANS

OLD AGE, NOT ENOUGH MONEY, NURSING HOME; THEN, SADLY YOU DIE

WHAT A PITY, WHAT A WASTE, THERE HAS TO BE A BETTER DREAM FOR ME

THE DREAM OF THE WISE

GO TO COLLEGE AND GET A GOOD EDUCATION

GRADUATE & CREATE/START YOUR OWN BUSINESS

GET MARRIED, IF YOU WISH AND INVEST IN REAL ESTATE

BUY YOUR DREAM HOME CASH WITH INVESTMENT EARNINGS

HAVE OTHERS WORKING FOR YOU & OBTAIN EXTREME WEALTH

LET YOUR BEING HERE CAUSE THE WORLD TO BE A BETTER PLACE

HELP PEOPLE,   DONATE TO WORTHY CAUSES & MAKE A DIFFERENCE

AT THE END, GOD CAN SAY WELL DONE MY GOOD AND FAITHFUL SERVANT

IT'S YOUR TIME NOW TO SEIZE THE MOMENT

*Right now, this very moment, is the greatest and most wonderful time to be alive. Whether you're **POOR, MIDDLE CLASS or RICH** doesn't matter; for today can be the day you start planting your seeds of wealth. Sure, it's going to take some time before you can honestly say "I'M RICH"; however, now you know how to do it. You've finally been blessed with the knowledge of how to get it done; and all that's left is for you to go out there and do it. I wish you well on your new and exciting journey to wealth and riches.*

Here's a serious word of warning to you, watch out for your friends and family members who will not understand your most recently found "unwavering desire to be RICH". They will try to discourage you because they will not be able to understand your motivation or your motives. This change that has taken place in your life will force a need for change in their lives; of which, they may not be willing to accept or able to adapt. All humans experience some stress having to do with change; while change can be good, it is not always easily accepted or welcomed. In this case, however, you might suggest that your friends and relatives read this book and hopefully, they too, will be able to see the wisdom.

However, if not, in order to follow your dream without out-side impediments or hindrances you may need to express your anxiety thusly:

"I think you are a great person. You have been a very good and loyal friend or family member and I truly care about you very much; however, I want to be RICH and it appears that you are okay with being where you are. Therefore, unless you can change your current attitude as it relates to money, prosperity & financial responsibility, I'm afraid that you may impede my progress. If you want to continue as my good friend or family member, I need us to be headed in the same or at least a similar direction. This is nothing personal; it's just business." Now, I must hurry for I have no time to waste. You see time is money and it's all about money. It always has been and it will always be about money. Those who have and those who have not make up this great land in which we live. I want to have. I want to be blessed. I want to be rich beyond my wildest dream. Don't you want that too?

THINGS YOU MUST ALWAYS REMEMBER

Money is the answer to all things. The pursuit of money is noble and wise.

Most people will earn a fortune in their lifetimes and still die poor; proving that it matters not how much money one earns, but how much one keeps of that which is earned. To save is wise and blessed.

Life's not promised to anyone. Live today and love someone. Don't live life so critical. Make room for a miracle.

God is waiting to assist you in your accomplishments and in the achievement of anything or any dream that you wish to pursue. With Him all things are possible and achievable.

It is God's divine will and desire that all of His children, which include you, have life and have it more abundantly.

As God' blesses you with wealth and riches, you must also bless others and pass on the WISDOM FOR CREATING WEALTH that you have learned and acquired along the way. Blessing others is the secret to motivating God ("THE GIVER" of all good and perfect things) to open the Windows of Heaven and pour out to you a blessing that you have not room to receive. To be blessed, you need only to follow the next (3) STEPS which profile the secrets for accumulating wealth.

MONEY, LIKE A FRUIT TREE PLANT, NEEDS TIME AND NOURISHMENT TO PRODUCE FRUIT, SO THE EARLIER YOU START PLANTING YOUR SEEDS OF WEALTH, THE SOONER AND RICHER WILL BE YOUR HARVEST.

THE SECRETS TO ACCUMULATING WEALTH SIMPLIFIED:

STEP 1

PLANTING THE SEEDS OF MONEY (BLESSINGS)

PAYING YOURSELF FIRST

MAKING YOUR DWELLING A PROFITABLE INVESTMENT

BUYING ASSETS: INCOME PROPERTY, LAND, STOCKS, MUTUAL FUNDS & etc.

HAVING AN UNWAVERING DESIRE TO BE RICH

STARTING YOUR OWN BUSINESS

STEP 2

CULTIVATING & NURTURING THE MONEY TREE
(BLESSING TREE)

CONTROLLING YOUR EXPENDITURES

INSURING A FUTURE INCOME

INCREASING YOUR ABILITY TO EARN

SEEKING WISE COUNSEL

GUARDING YOUR MONEY FROM LOSS

STEP 3

REAPING THE HARVEST (MONEY/BLESSINGS)!!!!
LEAPING & PRAISING!!!!!

MAKING YOUR MONEY WORK FOR YOU

PAYING CASH & NEGOTIATING PRICE

HAVING OTHERS WORKING FOR YOU

GIVING TOWARDS GOD'S WORK & BLESSING OTHERS

MONEY IS QUITE PLENTIFUL TO THOSE WHO UNDERSTAND THE *RULES* OF ITS ACQUISITION

7 RULES OF MONEY ACQUISITION

1. **PAY YOURSELF FIRST 10% OF YOUR GROSS INCOME**

2. **MAKE YOUR DWELLING A PROFITABLE INVESTMENT**

3. **MAKE YOUR MONEY WORK FOR YOU EVERY DAY**

4. **MAINTAIN AN UNWAVERING DESIRE AND PASSION FOR THE PURSUIT OF MONEY**

5. **CONTROL YOUR EXPENDITURES AND BE A SAVER**

6. **INCREASE YOUR ABILITY TO EARN AND INSURE A FUTURE INCOME FOR YOURSELF AND YOUR FAMILY**

7. **GUARD YOUR MONEY FROM LOSS AND SEEK WISE COUNSEL FROM COMPETENT AND WEALTHY PEOPLE**

(7) LAWS OF MONEY

1. Money answers all things. Give 10% of it towards God's work.

2. Money is plentiful to those who understand the simple rules of its acquisition.

3. Money comes quickly and easily to the one who pays himself first and buys assets to create a secure future for himself and his family.

4. Money works hard twenty-four hours per day, seven days per week; growing rapidly for one who finds it profitable and safe investments.

5. Money clings to those who will seek wise counsel and advice from competent & wealthy persons who know much about money matters.

6. Money flees from those who do <u>not</u> pay themselves first and those who follow the advice of "GET-RICH-QUICK" tricksters and schemers.

7. Money, like a fruit tree plant, needs time and nourishment to produce fruit, so the earlier you start planting your seeds of wealth, the sooner and richer will be your harvest.

NOW THAT YOU ARE ARMED WITH THE WISDOM AND THE KNOWLEDGE THAT YOU WILL NEED TO BECOME RICH AND WEALTHY, CAN YOU BE COUNTED ON TO USED IT, AND THEN PASS IT ON TO OTHERS?

ONCE YOU GET TO THE TOP,
DON'T FORGET TO
SEND THE ELEVATOR BACK DOWN

When you have achieved wealth and riches, don't forget to help someone else get there too. There is enough room for us all.

Helping others is the greatest gift anyone can give to humanity and the greatest and most elegant gift one can give to God. Helping others is also the easiest and most praiseworthy way to earn favor from God. Blessing others motivates God to bless you. Therefore, if you truly want to be blessed, just bless someone else.

This book is our sincere attempt at sending the elevator back down, and my humble desire to help someone as I continue to be abundantly blessed by God. Miss Donna and I wish you the very best that life offers. May God bless each of you with financial abundance and great joy is our prayer.

Abraham Brown & Donna Gordon-Brown

THE DEBT TERMINATOR
AND WEALTH ACCUMULATOR

SHARE IT WITH OTHERS

 Phone/fax orders: Call: 330 659- 3837 or Fax: 330- 659-9248

 E-mail orders: Order @ www.debtterminatorbook.com

 Postal orders: Send and make money orders payable to:
Abraham Brown
P. O. Box 34
Richfield, Ohio 44286
Phone: 330-659-3837 or Fax: 330-659-9248

-----------------------------CUT HERE--------------------------------

To order copies by fax or mail, use the order form below:

<u>U.S. $9.95 Canada $13.95</u> **(THE DEBT TERMINATOR** & *WEALTH ACCUMULATOR)*

_____ **Order Quantity** *(Qty. of 30 or more = 30% discount)*

_____ **Shipping & Handling**
U.S. *$4.95 first book & $2.00 for each Add'l. book.*
International: *$8.95 first book & $3.00 for ea. Add'l.*

_____ **Total Enclosed /Method of Payment** _____